A Teaching Assistant's Guide to Child Development and Psychology in the Classroom

How can you help students most effectively in the classroom? As a teaching assistant, you play a vital role in today's schools. This fully updated new edition will help you get to grips with the main issues to do with psychology and its role in the processes of teaching and learning.

This accessible text, building on the success of a bestselling previous edition, provides informative yet down-to-earth commentary with clear examples of how you can apply this knowledge in everyday practice.

The book addresses issues including how to:

- support learning
- identify and cater for different learning styles
- teach children with additional needs
- manage behaviour to support learning, and
- help children with their self-esteem and independence.

This new edition includes references to up-to-date research in child development and psychology about personalized learning, creativity, motivation, friendships skills, moral development and neuroscience. The information presented is complemented with lively case studies, self-assessment questions and examples of how to apply theory to everyday classroom practice. The reader is encouraged to develop reflective practice to best support children's behaviour and learning.

This reader-friendly book is an invaluable companion for every teaching assistant, higher level teaching assistant, cover supervisor or anyone working in a supporting role in an educational setting.

Susan Bentham is Senior Lecturer in Education at the University of Chichester. She is the author of *A Teaching Assistant's Guide to Managing Behaviour in the Classroom* and guides for teaching assistants to complete NVQ Levels 2 and 3 (all published by Routledge).

A Teaching Assistant's Guide to Child Development and Psychology in the Classroom

Second edition

Susan Bentham

RECEIVED

AUG 2 3 2011

MINNESOTA STATE UNIVERSITY
MANKATO, MN 56002-8419

Routledge
Taylor & Francis Group

LONDON AND NEW YORK

First edition published 2004
by RoutledgeFalmer

This edition published 2011
by Routledge
2 Park Square, Milton Park, Abingdon, Oxon, OX14 4RN

Simultaneously published in the USA and Canada
by Routledge
711 Third Avenue, New York, NY 10017

*Routledge is an imprint of the Taylor & Francis Group, an
informa business*

© 2004, 2011 Susan Bentham

All rights reserved. No part of this book may be
reprinted or reproduced or utilised in any form or
by any electronic, mechanical, or other means, now
known or hereafter invented, including photocopying
and recording, or in any information storage or retrieval
system, without permission in writing from the
publishers.

Trademark notice: Product or corporate names may be
trademarks or registered trademarks, and are used only
for identification and explanation without intent to
infringe.

British Library Cataloguing in Publication Data
A catalogue record for this book is available from the
British Library

Library of Congress Cataloging-in-Publication Data
Bentham, Susan, 1958-
A teaching assistant's guide to child development and
psychology in the classroom / Susan Bentham. — 2nd
ed.
   p.cm.
   Includes bibliographical references and index.
   1. Child development—Handbooks, manuals, etc. 2.
Child psychology—Handbooks, manuals, etc. 3. Teachers'
assistants—Handbooks, manuals, etc. I. Title.
   LB1117.B465 2011
   302.231—dc22   2010037330

ISBN13: 978-0-415-56922-4 (hbk)
ISBN13: 978-0-415-56923-1 (pbk)
ISBN13: 978-0-203-82948-6 (ebk)

Typeset in Bembo by
Pindar NZ, Auckland, New Zealand
Printed and bound in Great Britain by
TJ International Ltd, Padstow, Cornwall

LB
1117
.B465
2011

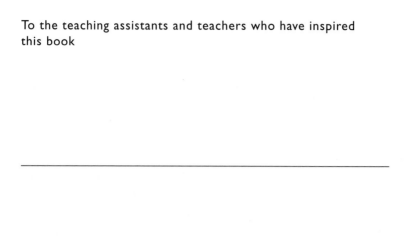

To the teaching assistants and teachers who have inspired this book

Contents

Illustrations

Figures

Tables

Case studies

Acknowledgements

A very special thank you to my son, Matthew – for his great artwork!

Introduction

The first edition of this book was written in 2003; however, as so much has changed in the field of education in the intervening years, a new edition is needed.

In 2004 *Every Child Matters* was published, with its emphasis on inclusion and giving all children the support they need to be healthy and stay safe, enjoy learning, be able to make a positive contribution to society, and achieve economic well-being. There have also been initiatives such as the Primary National Strategy and policies on personalized learning, creativity and assessment for learning, to mention just a few.

And of course there has been the National Agreement (DfES 2003), which was designed to raise pupils' standards and tackle teacher workload through giving teaching assistants (TAs) additional responsibilities and duties and by creating new support roles such as the Higher Level Teaching Assistant (HLTA). As a consequence of the National Agreement, TAs may now find themselves involved in keeping records, setting up classroom displays and invigilating examinations.

Government statistics (DfES 2006) put the number of TAs employed in schools to be equivalent to 153,000 full-time staff. Furthermore, there are additional support roles in schools, including after-school supervisors, cover supervisors and midday-meal supervisors. What remains constant is the incredibly valuable work that teaching assistants and support workers do on a daily basis in schools. This book has been written for all individuals in schools who are involved in supporting teaching and learning.

The aim of this book is to give readers an understanding of the basic concepts relating to child development and psychology. Knowledge of such issues is interesting in itself, but the support staff with whom I have worked want also to know how they can use this information in the classroom to better support the pupils.

This book gives many examples of how theories and concepts can both explain pupil behaviour and be used to support learning. Here the word 'learning' is used in its most general sense to mean acquiring academic, behavioural and social skills.

Above all, this book aims to be reader-friendly and practical. However, there is a lot of terminology in child development and psychology, so whenever new terminology first occurs in this book it is highlighted in bold type and explained within the text. In addition, definitions of key concepts can be found in the glossary. Terminology can seem overwhelming at first, but a grasp of such terms can be extremely useful when communicating with other teaching professionals.

An important feature of this book is its emphasis on reflection. Throughout each chapter exercises and case studies reinforce key concepts, give examples of how theory can be applied to practice, and ask questions that will encourage the reader to think deeply or reflect about their own practice.

Definitions of reflection and the reflective practitioner

Reflection is a word that is often used in the field of education. As teachers are encouraged to be reflective practitioners, so too are those involved in supporting teaching and learning. But what is reflection and what is a reflective practitioner? And more to the point, how does reflection relate to what teaching assistants and support workers in school do on a daily basis?

Reflection has been defined as a 'kind of thinking that consists in turning a subject over in the mind and giving it serious thought' (Dewey 1933). The subject in this case is your working day. At the end of a working day you might want to go home, put your feet up, enjoy a soothing drink of your choice and forget. But perhaps your mind can't switch off and your thoughts wander back to something that happened at school, some incident that went really well or perhaps something that did not go quite as you had hoped. Reflection starts with replaying an event in your mind. The purpose of replaying the event is to try to understand or make sense of what happened. Reflection involves asking questions about the events that happen and specifically thinking about your ideas, feelings, beliefs and values.

Sometimes thinking alone is not enough to help you understand or make sense of what happened – sometimes you need to talk to others about what happened. You might need to ask for advice. Sometimes asking ourselves questions can be unsettling, and it is helpful to have a critical friend to whom we can turn for advice and who can help us to see more clearly. The hope is that through reflection, i.e. through seriously thinking about what you do and how you do it, you will become better at what you do. When you start the process of thinking about *how you do what you do* on a regular basis, you are well on your way to becoming a reflective practitioner. So, to summarize:

- Reflection is part of the process of making sense of what happens to us.
- Reflection involves thinking and asking ourselves questions.
- A critical friend to whom we can talk and seek advice from can help us see more clearly.
- Reflecting and learning from our experiences can enable us to better support the pupils we work with.
- Those involved in the teaching profession need to continually engage in reflection and thereby work at becoming reflective practitioners.

It has been said that reflection requires us to engage with the past, the present and the future. Many of the TAs with whom I have worked have described their own experiences of school as challenging and sometimes incredibly difficult. But these experiences, rather than putting them off, have – in the TAs' words – given them greater empathy for the pupils with whom they work and a real desire to make a difference. At this point, it may be useful to reflect on your own learning journey, and how your experiences of learning impact on your ability to support teaching and learning.

Thinking deeply

Draw a line depicting your life (past, present and future) and mark an X for where you are now.

Reflect upon your experiences of learning. You might want to consider:
   What were your experiences at school?
   How did you feel about your teachers?
   Who was your favourite teacher and why?
   Which teachers did you find difficult and why?
   Which subjects did you enjoy and why?
   The next questions are more difficult:
   How have your experiences of learning in the past influenced your ability to support learners in the present? For example, do you think your experience of learning has made you more empathetic towards the pupils you are working with?
   How does thinking about your past experiences of learning influence how you hope to support pupils in the future?

Ways to reflect: the reflective account

Reflection sounds interesting but how do you start? First it is helpful to write your thoughts down because the process of writing can help to clarify your thoughts. This can take the form of a diary or a *reflective personal account*. When writing down what has happened, it is helpful to structure your thoughts. One way of writing down your thoughts has been devised by Gibbs (1988: 52) who talks of a reflective cycle. This cycle is as follows:

- *Description of event*. State what happened. Sometimes it may be helpful to write down what should have happened.
- *Feelings*. What were you thinking and feeling? Perhaps you could also add how you thought the pupils were thinking and feeling. It might be helpful to consider how confident you felt in the situation.
- *Evaluation*. What was difficult about the event? What was good about the event?

It is important to realize that evaluation is not always negative. If a lesson with a pupil has gone really well then you will want to know what it was that made that lesson effective so you can use that approach again. However, it is also true that sometimes in life we actually learn more when things don't go the way we had planned.

- *Analysis*. How do you make sense of what has happened? Why do you think this happened? Has anything similar happened to you before? Can any psychological and educational theories explain what happened?

As you find out more about psychology and child development, you will be able to use this information to help you to reflect.

- *In conclusion*. What else could you have done?
- *Action plan*. If the event occurs again, what would you do differently? What can you do to feel more confident in such situations?

This outline of a reflective account is a cycle because there is never an end to reflecting. The action plan leads on to the next event, which leads to the next cycle of questioning. At this point you might be saying that this seems too much like hard work and that you don't often think about what you do, you just do it. In the next few pages we will look at various ways of reflecting.

Case study 0.1

The reflective account

Wendy, a teaching assistant in a primary school, was on playground duty. Wendy describes the following incident:

> I noticed James playing on the grass area behind the fence. As it is an out-of-bounds area, I went up to James and asked him to leave the area and come back with me to the playground. He refused to leave. He shouted: 'I don't have to do what you say!' I took his hand and expected him to come with me, but he then fell to the ground and started making faces. I asked him again to come back to the playground and he told me to 'F★★★ off'. Another child that I knew was nearby and I asked that child to go and tell the Deputy Head who was also on playground duty what was happening. I tried again to coax James back into the playground, but now he started screaming. Miss Murphy, the Deputy Head, arrived at this point and thanked me for my involvement and told me to go back to the playground. Miss Murphy told James very firmly that she had had enough of his nonsense and to get up and to go back with her. James got up and went into the playground with Miss Murphy.

To make sense of this event Wendy wrote her thoughts down within the framework of a reflective account.

Reflective account

Name	Wendy Lawson
Description of event What happened? and/or What should have happened?	I was on playground duty. One child was in the out-of-bounds area. When I asked him to leave, he refused, fell to the ground and was abusive. I asked another child to go and fetch the Deputy Head. She thanked me for my involvement and quickly dealt with the child.
Feelings What did I feel? What did the pupil/pupils feel?	I know I did the right thing in calling for assistance, but I felt that I should have really been able to cope with the situation by myself. Even though I have been working in the school for over a year now, I still don't always feel confident in dealing with children who are disruptive. As for James, well, he was very upset. I just don't know what got in to him, as he is usually a cooperative child.

(continued)

Reflective account (continued)

Name	Wendy Lawson
Evaluation What was good? What was difficult?	What was good about the event was that the situation was sorted and that the Deputy Head brought James back into the school grounds. It was good that I took action to get backup from the Deputy Head. What was difficult about the event? Well, I feel maybe if I had acted differently I would have been able to handle the situation.
Analysis How do I make sense of this? Why did this happen?	I don't know why James behaved in this manner.
In conclusion What else could I have done?	What else could I have done? Well I actually spent a lot of time thinking about this. In the end I felt I was going nowhere so I decided to talk to my friend Sheila who is also a teaching assistant. Sheila has been at the school for over five years. She suggested that maybe I should have asked him why he was in the out-of-bounds area in the first place. I never thought to ask him that. Sheila said that she had noticed that earlier in the day there had seemed to be some sort of fight between James and his best friend, Sam. Perhaps if I had asked James why he was there, he might not have thrown himself down on the ground. Sheila also suggested that I go to the Deputy Head and ask her for her advice. Maybe the Deputy Head has some tips on behaviour management.
Action plan Next time I would . . .	What would I do next time? Perhaps I should keep an extra eye on that area and actually remind pupils who are getting too close to the area that they need to move somewhere else rather than wait till they are out of bounds and then have to tell them off. What can I do to feel more confident? That is a very difficult question. The Deputy Head has offered to find me some handouts on managing disruptive behaviour. But what has helped my confidence has been talking about this to Sheila and the Deputy Head.

Thinking deeply

The reflective account outlines how Wendy made sense of the event, but how would you make sense of the event?

Can you think of any other explanations to explain James's behaviour?

Can you think of any other ways to deal with James's behaviour?

Do you think it helped Wendy to write a reflective account? If so, how? If not, why not?

Ways to reflect: the professional dialogue

Case study 0.2

The professional dialogue

Chris is a teaching assistant in a large secondary school. Chris was working in a Year 9 science class, playing a game with seven pupils. The game was a sort of Trivial Pursuit game that tested the pupils' knowledge on key facts that they would need to know for their upcoming test. Chris was being observed by Mary, the school's Higher level teaching assistant (HLTA). At the end of the class, Chris went back to the learning support unit and had an informal chat with Mary. She explained that their discussion would be an opportunity for Chris to reflect on her practice within the classroom.

Mary: How did you think the session went?

Chris: Well, on the whole I think it went very well. My task as set out by the teacher was to play a revision game. The teacher told me what pupils I would be working with and for the entire session we played the game. I think that it was a very enjoyable and useful session. The pupils must have enjoyed the session, as they wanted to play it again. However, two pupils did wander off to do something else, so maybe they didn't enjoy the game and there were a few problems at the beginning. Of course, as you know, there was an argument between these two lads about who was to start first and it took a while to sort that out. In the end I decided who was going to start. However, the game went well and most of the pupils asked if they could play the game next lesson, so they must have really enjoyed it.

Mary: So you are saying that you had some difficulties starting the task and some difficulties keeping all pupils engaged with the game. What would you do differently next time?

Chris: Well, I think I should have had a clear plan about who should have started first; for instance, whoever throws the highest number on the dice. As it was, I just simply asked who wants to start first and that started the argument. As for the two pupils who wandered off, I went up to them later and asked why. They just shrugged their shoulders and said it was boring. But I was wondering if maybe some of the questions were just too difficult for them and they just didn't want to be shown up in front of their friends. Next time I think I would definitely have a range of questions to ask, starting with some easy ones.

Mary: I think those are very good ideas and that they would make a difference to the pupils' learning. However, what struck me was your use of questions.

Chris: I don't understand what you are getting at. It was a game of Trivial Pursuit. I asked them the question and if they didn't know the answer, I told them.

Mary: Do you think that you gave them enough time to answer the question?

Chris: Perhaps I was rushing them a bit – but we had a lot of questions to get through.

Mary: Do you think reading out the answers will help them to remember the answers?

Chris: I can see your point.

Mary   What else could you have done?

Chris: Given them more time?

Mary: Yes, but perhaps you could have given them prompts or hints or encouraged other pupils to give prompts or hints. Then all pupils would have been involved in all stages of the game and not just when it was their turn.

Chris: That's a good idea.

Afterwards Chris discussed the observation and professional dialogue, which was the formal discussion she had had with Mary about the lesson, with the other TAs at break time. What impressed Chris was that although she had reflected on what had happened, having someone else to reflect with gave her a completely different perspective on what had happened.

Thinking deeply

Consider Chris's account of the Year 9 science class. Can you think of any other explanations to explain why the pupils wandered off from the game?

Can you think of any other ways to help the pupils engage with the game?

If you had observed Chris, what questions would you have asked?

Final comments

If you have done the 'thinking deeply' questions, you will have probably come up with alternative reasons for why James was in the out-of-bounds area or why Chris's pupils wandered off from the revision game. You might have come up with other ideas or ways to deal with James or how to keep Chris's pupils interested in the science game. There is no one right answer. Reflection involves coming up with possible ideas that will keep pupils on track and ideas that will enable them to learn more effectively. Reflection involves experimentation, i.e. trying out ideas and seeing what works. What the second example shows is that reflection can be enhanced by discussing your ideas with others. Remember a critical friend with whom you can talk and seek advice from, can help you to see more clearly.

Figure 1 Humpty Dumpty needed encouragement from his critical friend to overcome his fear of climbing. Choose your critical friend with care.

Reflection is not easy! Reflection requires serious thinking. But hope-fully what these examples and your own consideration of these events has shown is that thinking or reflecting about situations leads to a greater understanding of the situation and generates ideas about how to become better at what you do.

Chapter 1

Basic principles underlying pupil development and learning

This chapter outlines how individuals develop and learn. We know from experience that there is a world of difference between what a three-year-old toddler can do compared with a thirteen-year-old adolescent. The big question that various theorists have attempted to explain is: How does this change occur?

Many theorists talk about stages of development, i.e. they outline what the average child can do at a certain age and how the behaviour of this average child changes through time. Now while this approach is useful in suggesting what to expect at certain ages, we also know that even children of the same age can differ widely in terms of what they can and cannot do. In fact there is no such animal as the 'average child'. However, if a child is behaving in a manner that is considerably different from what we would expect, then this could indicate some underlying issue. (For further information on children with additional needs, see Chapter 4.)

What we will also discover is that different theorists have different views. But if debate exists, you might want to ask: What is the right view? However, there is no *one* right view – all theories offer some insights into how individuals develop and learn. The fact that debate exists highlights the complexity of learning and development.

Intellectual and cognitive skills

Piaget

In everyday language, when we say someone is intellectual we are saying that we think they are very clever or smart. But what do we mean by clever? In part, intellectual ability is due to cognitive skills, i.e. how someone thinks and reasons through ideas and problems. Jean Piaget (1896–1980) devoted his adult life to the study of **cognitive development**, i.e. how individuals learn to think and how thinking develops over time. Piaget was interested in tracking how thinking develops from a newborn infant, through the 'terrible twos', to the pupil just beginning school, to the lanky adolescent, and finally onwards to the emerging adult. Piaget studied thinking by observing children doing specific tasks and by asking them specific questions. For example, Piaget was interested in how children came to understand why some objects float in water whereas others sink. Piaget was interested in how children would solve such problems as: 'If Amy is taller than Susan and Sarah is shorter than Susan, then who is the taller: Amy or Sarah?'

One of Piaget's greatest insights started with the awareness that a child's manner of thinking is very different from that of an adult, that thinking changes with time, and that these changes are both quantitative and qualitative. Quantitative refers to the amount of thinking, while qualitative refers to the style or manner in which we think.

Cognitive development, according to Piaget, was due to an interaction between the developing individual and the individual's experience within the environment. Piaget believed that children were little scientists who constructed or created knowledge by being actively involved in what was going on around them. Children learned best by discovering things for themselves. However, what children can learn is limited by their age. A thirteen-year-old can be taught algebra, but a two-year-old can't. Children of four or five can begin to learn to read. But can you teach an eighteen-month-old child to read? Piaget labelled this as **maturational readiness**. At a certain age a child's thinking ability develops to a point that makes it possible for a child to learn certain skills. Obviously this has important implications for when certain skills are taught in schools. Piaget went on to describe *how* individuals learn new information. Central to Piaget's theory is the concept of **schemas**. Schemas are units of mental thought. Schemas have been compared to files in which we store information. But how do schemas develop in the first place? To answer this question Piaget outlined a process called **adaptation**, which involved **assimilation** and **accommodation**. This sounds quite complex but the following case study illustrates how this terminology can relate to everyday experiences.

Case study 1.1

Developing an understanding of shape

Imagine a primary maths classroom. The teaching assistant is working with two pupils (Sam and Kylie) on shape, in particular the difference between squares and rectangles. Each child has in front of them ten shapes: five squares and five rectangles of varying size and colour. The task is to sort the shapes into piles of squares and rectangles.

Kylie knows that squares have four sides and so have rectangles, but squares are different from rectangles in that all four sides are the same length. Kylie looks at all the shapes and is a little bit confused by the fact that some shapes are bigger than others, but then she remembers that for a shape to be a square it must have four sides of equal length, so it does not matter if some squares are bigger than others. Kylie also knows that rectangles do not have sides of equal length. Kylie correctly sorts the shapes into squares and rectangles. Kylie has taken this new information regarding different sizes of squares and rectangles and fitted it, or assimilated it, into her existing understanding of what squares and rectangles are.

Sam, however, has problems with this task. He quickly sorts the shapes out into two piles corresponding to big shapes and small shapes. The teaching assistant asks him where are the squares. Sam says all the shapes are squares. The teaching assistant asks him where are the rectangles. Sam says all the shapes are rectangles. Sam adds all the shapes are the same because they have four corners. The teaching assistant tries to explain that there is a difference between squares and rectangles. Sam looks upset as he realizes he has got it wrong. Here Sam has an existing schema about shape that states squares and rectangles are the same as they have four corners. Sam is correct but there are also differences between squares and rectangles. Sam's understanding of squares and rectangles is not the same as society's shared understanding of what is a square and what is a rectangle. Sam is experiencing what Piaget would term **cognitive disequilibrium**. Sam realizes sadly that how he understands squares and rectangles is not the same as everyone else. According to Piaget, this state of cognitive disequilibrium is unpleasant and that will motivate Sam to try to figure out the difference between a square and a rectangle. Sam needs to create a new schema for squares and rectangles. The process of creating new schemas is called **accommodation**.

Thinking deeply

What possible explanations are there for Sam's lack of understanding?
  How would you support Sam?
  Why would simply telling Sam the answer NOT be helpful?
  How would you respond to Sam being sad and upset?

To summarize:

- Schemas are units of mental thought.
- Adaptation explains the process of learning.
- Adaptation involves both assimilation and accommodation.
- Assimilation is when you take new information and fit it into an existing schema or file.
- When new experiences cannot fit into existing schemas or files then an unpleasant state of cognitive disequilibrium is said to exist.
- In order to put an end to this state of cognitive disequilibrium, the individual must create new schemas, through a process called accommodation.

It is important to note that being in a state of cognitive disequilibrium, i.e. realizing that you are confused and that you don't understand, may not always result in greater motivation to find the right answer. A pupil experiencing these feelings might simply give up. Recent research has focused on the relationship between how pupils approach difficulties in learning and the importance of viewing 'mistakes' as a vital part of the learning process. More will be said about this in Chapter 7.

Figure 2 'My husband says he can't do the dishes or mow the lawn because he's not maturationally ready!'

Piaget also believed that development occurs in four stages. These stages are universal: everyone goes through these stages in the same order and at no time can an individual skip or miss stages. Although Piaget stated corresponding ages for various stages, he did note that there could be variation, i.e. some children would enter the stage earlier and some children would enter the stage later. Piaget's four stages will now be described.

Sensori-motor stage (birth to two years)

The achievements of this stage are **object permanence** and **general symbolic function**. Object permanence is the awareness that something exists in time and space even if we cannot see it. For example, does a young child realize that teddy still exists even if teddy is put away in the toy box? The classic test for this is to fully cover a toy with a cloth while a baby is watching. The important part is that the baby sees you hide the toy. Will the baby search and find the toy or will the baby act as though 'out of sight is out of mind'? Surprisingly it is not until eight to twelve months that a baby will actively search for and find a toy that they have seen being hidden.

General symbolic function includes the emergence of language, make-believe play and **deferred imitation**. Deferred imitation is an important skill, which starts with watching someone else; in particular, watching what a person does and noting exactly what happens to that person. Deferred imitation then involves deliberating or thinking about whether the behaviour viewed was worth repeating. If the behaviour was seen as worthwhile, the individual waits and, when an opportunity arises, remembers the initial behaviour and then copies that behaviour. For example, John is twenty months and an only child. When John is good his mother gives him a chocolate biscuit, which she keeps in a cupboard well out of his reach. One day John's three-year-old cousin comes to visit. John's mother gives them both biscuits. While the mothers are busy in another room, John watches as his cousin goes into the kitchen, moves a chair, climbs onto the chair and then onto the counter, opens the cupboard and gets another biscuit. The next day, John's mother walks into the kitchen to find John standing on the counter eating a chocolate biscuit. This, according to Piaget, is an example of deferred imitation.

Pre-operational stage (two to seven years)

This stage sees an amazing growth in the use of language and the beginnings of problem solving. Children begin to develop concepts such as: How many? How much does it weigh? How tall is it? What time is it? However, children at this age are limited in their logical thinking because, according to Piaget, they are egocentric and unable to decentre. **Egocentrism**, or being **egocentric**, involves the child believing that others see the world as they do. The classic test for this is known as the three mountains test. The test goes like this:

1. The child is shown a three-dimensional model of three mountains: one with snow on it, one with a cabin on it and the last mountain with a cross on it. The child sits at one end of the table while a doll is placed at the other end of the table.
2. The child is then shown a series of pictures of the mountains taken from different perspectives.
3. The child is asked to select what picture best represents what they see and what picture best represents what the doll sees.

In order to do this task, the child needs to realize that because they are looking at the mountains from a different angle, what they see is different from what the doll sees. In addition, the child needs to visualize in their mind what the doll sees from the doll's position. This is a difficult test and it is not until about age nine that a child can accurately select the view that the doll sees.

When a child has the ability to see the world from another's perspective, Piaget would say they have the ability to decentre. To **decentre** involves the child holding and understanding two apparently opposing views in their mind at the same time. In the three mountains test, a child has decentred when they realize that what the doll sees is different from what they see because the doll is at the other end of the table.

Piaget was also interested in children's ability to **conserve**. Conservation involves the realization that an object remains the same even though its appearance changes. Piaget developed many tests to explore children's understanding of conservation. The conservation of number test goes like this:

The conservation of number test

Experimenter: (shows two identical lines of beads)

● ● ● ● ●

● ● ● ● ●

Experimenter: Do the two rows have the same number of beads?
Five-year-old child: Yes.
Experimenter: (rearranges one row by increasing the spaces between the beads)

● ● ● ● ●

● ● ● ● ●

Experimenter: Do the two rows have the same number of beads?
Five-year-old child: (points to the row with the greater spaces between the beads)
That row has more!

In this example, the child has been fooled by appearances – the second row looks longer so therefore it must have more beads. The child's failure to conserve can be explained by their inability to decentre, i.e. their inability to hold in their mind two apparently opposing views. It is not until about age six that a child will be able to reason that although the rows look different, nothing has changed. A six-year-old child might say: 'The rows are the same, they just look different. They still have the same number. You just moved them.'

Concrete operational stage (seven to eleven years)

Children at this stage are better at logical thinking. Children can now successfully answer questions relating to **transitivity**, a type of reasoning that can be illustrated by: 'If Amy is taller than Susan and Sarah is shorter than Susan, then who is the taller: Amy or Sarah?'

However, children in this stage are limited in regard to their logical thinking as they can only think about things that are actually present. An example to illustrate this point would involve asking children the question: 'If you had a third eye, where would you put it and why?' Typically children in this stage will place the third eye in the middle of their forehead between their existing eyes. Here the children are bound by the realities of the world, that eyes are located on a certain part of your face (Sigelman and Shaffer 1991). It is not until age eleven or twelve that children develop the skill of abstract thinking and can consider possibilities that contradict reality.

Figure 3 Where would you put a third eye? For Jason and his dad, the answer
seemed obvious.

Formal operational stage (eleven to twelve years and over)

This is the stage when children have developed the beginnings of abstract
thought. This is why algebra is not taught until a child is eleven or twelve.
Individuals of this age now engage in what is termed **hypothetical
deductive reasoning**. This involves generating a hypothesis, stating the
implications of the hypothesis, testing the hypothesis, drawing conclusions,
and finally generating or coming up with yet more hypotheses.

To summarize

For Piaget, cognitive development is due to an interaction between the
developing child and the child's experience within the environment. Piaget
stated that the newly acquired knowledge is stored in the form of schemas or units of mental thought. Schemas are in turn formed through the
processes of assimilation and accommodation. Piaget believed that children progress through four stages of cognitive development. The first stage,
sensori-motor (birth to two years), is characterized by the development of

object permanence, language, make-believe play and deferred imitation. In the second stage, pre-operational (two to seven years), the child's thinking lacks logic, and the child can be fooled by the ways things look, e.g. if an object looks like it is bigger, then it must be bigger. The child also has difficulty in stating how what they see is different from what other people would see. This is illustrated in Piaget's three mountains test. In the third stage, concrete operational (seven to eleven years), the child can use logic, but only on objects that are actually present. The final and fourth stage, formal operational (eleven to twelve or more years), sees the development of abstract thought.

Vygotsky

Vygotsky was a Russian theorist who wrote on education, sociology, art, history and philosophy. Although Vygotsky died in 1933, his views on education are still very influential today. Vygotsky emphasized the importance of social interactions in cognitive development. If we remember, Piaget saw children as young scientists discovering knowledge for themselves through being actively involved in the world around them. However, Vygotsky stated that being actively involved was not enough – for learning to happen, Vygotsky believed that children need to be engaged in talking with others about what they were supposed to be learning and, specifically, they need support and guidance from someone more experienced in regard to how to learn.

One of Vygotsky's key ideas concerned what he termed the **Zone of Proximal Development** (ZPD). The Zone of Proximal Development outlines both what the pupil can do by themselves and what they can do with the help of a more experienced person. Vygotsky believed that:

• What a pupil can do today with assistance, the pupil will in time be able to do by themselves.
• What a pupil can do with assistance is always more than what they can do by themselves.

This approach stresses the role of the more experienced person and the language of communication. Vygotsky coined the term **scaffolding**. Scaffolding is a process where through talking, a more skilled individual is trying to impart their knowledge to a less skilled individual. Effective communication involves the pupil and teacher coming to a shared understanding. In case study 1.1, Sam did not know the difference between a square and a rectangle; the teaching assistant needed to explain to Sam the difference in such a way that (and this is the hard part) Sam's understanding of a rectangle and square would become the same as her understanding.

Vygotsky and Piaget had different views in regard to maturational readiness, i.e. at what age, or stage of development, a child would be ready to learn new knowledge. For example, if a pupil had difficulty understanding a concept, e.g. the difference between a square and a rectangle, Piaget would say that:

- The pupil would need to discover the concept for themselves; in this case, by exploring different shapes.
- If the pupil could not grasp or understand the concept then their mind was just not ready to understand, but in time, when their mind had developed sufficiently, then they would be able to understand.

Vygotsky, however, believed that thinking and understanding was developed through communication and dialogue and, therefore, rather than wait for the thinking processes to mature, thinking and understanding could be brought on by the effective use of scaffolding. (For further information on scaffolding, see Chapter 2.)

The behaviourist view

Behaviourists believe that an individual's behaviour is controlled or determined by what happens to them in the environment. Behaviour can be explained by the principles of reinforcement and punishment. Simply put, behaviourists believe that:

- If behaviour is rewarded or reinforced then the behaviour will increase. A reward will always result in an increase in the behaviour.
- If behaviour is punished then the behaviour will decrease. A punishment will always result in a decrease in the behaviour.

This theory is deceptively simple as what is considered a punishment and what is considered a reward depends very much on the individual.

However, it is important to note that in schools we no longer talk of doling out punishments; rather we administer considered sanctions in line with school policies. Consider the following:

Case study 1.2

Is it a sanction – or a reward?

James is in a Year 10 maths class. James hates maths and he hates his teacher, who he feels is always having a go at him. Today James has brought a beetle into class. When the teacher discovers the beetle on James's desk, the teacher insists that James remove the beetle at once. James says that the beetle is his best friend and that he will not stay in class if his best friend can't. The other pupils find this very amusing. The teacher, needless to say, is not amused and sends James out. The teacher thought he was punishing James, i.e. administering an appropriate sanction, but James was thrilled because he would do anything to get out of maths.

What case study 1.2 shows is that for the pupil, being sent out of class was perceived not as punishment or appropriate sanction (as believed by the teacher) but as a reward. The teacher, without realizing it, was actually reinforcing, or rewarding, playing-up behaviour.

Figure 4 The way pupils view situations can be different from teaching professionals. In his mind, this is how James saw the situation.

Another approach to learning explains how individuals learn what is called **conditioned emotional responses**. This is a type of learning that results in certain events, situations and people being associated with particular emotions and feelings. When a person states that they have a fear of reading out loud and that fear can be traced back to some nasty experience that occurred when they were young, they are, without realizing it, talking about conditioned emotional responses. Conditioned emotional responses can be explained by **classical conditioning** and this is where it gets complicated. Classical conditioning involves associating the automatic reactions caused by one event to other events that just happened to be occurring at the same time. To understand this terminology, let's look at the following case study which details how one man learned to fear reading out loud.

Case study 1.3

Classical conditioning

Rodney is a fifty-five-year-old successful businessman. Rodney reminisces regarding his experiences at school.

> My school was very strict. I remember this one day in English. Mr Teddington singled me out and told me to stand up and read a passage from Dickens's book *Great Expectations*. Well, I didn't like reading out loud and I stumbled over my words. Mr Teddington glared at me and bellowed: 'You silly boy, read it again.' So I did, but I still made mistakes. He just said: 'You are going to read it until you get it right.' Well, I spent the next twenty minutes reading that passage. At the end I was shaking, sweating and on the verge of bursting into tears. Well, after that I was never any good at English. I hated going to English classes and to this day I still can't read out loud in front of groups.

This is quite an extreme example. However, Rodney's learned hatred of English classes and his learned fear of reading out loud in front of groups can be traced back to what happened in Mr Teddington's class and this can be analysed in classical conditioning terms.

What case study 1.3 illustrates is that for learning to be successful, learning must *not* be associated with negative emotional experiences because these negative experiences could be associated with the wider learning environment. Furthermore, although conditioned emotional responses may be learnt in one specific setting, they may linger in the soul and be triggered unexpectedly in another setting – as case study 1.4 illustrates.

Conditioned stimulus	elicits/leads to	Conditioned response
A stimulus which comes to elicit a response by being associated with another stimulus		A response elicited by a conditioned stimulus
(In case study 1.3, the conditioned stimulus is being in an English class and reading out loud to a group of people)		(In case study 1.3, the conditioned response is to associate fear and humiliation with being in an English class and reading out loud to a group of people)

Case study 1.4

A conditioned emotional response

I was supporting Alicia, a challenging but rather charming young pupil in English. This day we had a supply teacher, an older gentleman with lots of white curly hair and a strong local accent. As the lesson progressed I noticed that Alicia had become exceptionally quiet and pale. Then, as the supply teacher approached her, she screamed 'You B******', threw her books at him and ran out of the class. Obviously the behaviour was totally unacceptable. But later I found out that the supply teacher bore a striking resemblance to her stepdad, a man who, although currently in prison, had systematically abused her over many years. I suppose for Alicia the appearance of the supply teacher triggered all sorts of horrible memories and although she was safe in a classroom, in her mind she was with her stepdad. It seemed that for her the past and present had merged, and all the rage she felt towards her stepdad was literally thrown at the supply teacher.

Thinking deeply

How should the school respond to Alicia?
    How would you support Alicia?

The social learning approach

The social learning approach states that we learn by observing and imitating others. Simply put, observational learning can be described by the command to watch and learn. This view states that an individual can start to behave in a certain way without previously being rewarded for that behaviour. In this case, a person has watched how another person behaves and has observed what has happened to them in terms of being rewarded or punished. This relates to the ability which Piaget termed deferred imitation (see page 15). When psychologists talk about the dangers of children watching violent films, what they fear is that children will watch the aggression in films and then at some later point imitate this aggressive behaviour in real life. However, observational learning is an important part of the learning process because children can imitate both desirable and undesirable behaviour.

Albert Bandura (1977), an influential North American psychologist, felt that there were four component parts to observational learning:

1. *Attentional processes.* We cannot imitate others unless we first pay attention to what others are doing.
2. *Retentional processes.* As we may not imitate the behaviour for some time, we need a way of remembering, i.e. storing and organizing in our mind what we have seen.
3. *Motor reproduction processes.* This involves both remembering what to do and the necessity to practise the behaviour. For example, we might want to learn to ice skate. We might have watched skaters like Torville and Dean many times. However, the first time we put on skates and venture on to the ice we will not be able to imitate what they do.
4. *Motivational processes.* Although we have acquired knowledge of a behaviour, we do not necessarily imitate the behaviour. In other words, we see people do many things that we would not dream of imitating. So what leads to imitation? The motivation to imitate depends on whether we think we can perform the behaviour and what we think will happen to us if we do.

The person we imitate is called a model. The model might be an actual person (an admired classmate), or the model might be symbolic, such as a cartoon character (Bart Simpson) or a film character (Harry Potter). **Social learning theory** states that children are more likely to imitate:

- models who are similar to themselves, e.g. the same sex

- models who have been rewarded for their behaviour
- models who have power or status (strength, fame, special abilities).

New developments in thinking about learning: lessons from neuroscience

Neuroscience is the study of the nervous system and aims to explain behaviour in terms of activities in the brain. Much recent research has focused on how insights generated from this new exciting science can transform teaching. However, scientists caution that not all new ideas are supported by evidence and that there is a need to distinguish fact from fiction, or what is termed neuromyths. The concept of a programme being supported by evidence is an important one. To examine this, let's imagine the following situation.

Case study 1.5

A neuromyth?

Mandy and her teacher have found an article that states that in order to improve a pupil's attention and focus in class, then all you have to do is have the pupil tilt their head to the right; this simple action will release a certain chemical into their brain that will improve their ability to learn. Mandy and Mrs Smythe decide to try it out. The Head Teacher agrees that they can do this, but states that the idea is an example of pseudo-science which means, that while it sounds like it is scientific, it really isn't – there is no real evidence that tilting your head releases a chemical that enhances learning. Nevertheless, both Mandy and Mrs Smythe are very enthusiastic about this idea and want to try it out anyway. The children in the class are also excited when they hear what just tilting their head can do and are eager to try it, too. So now every time the pupils are about to start a new piece of work, they all are quiet, tilt their head to the right and think nice thoughts for three minutes. And you know, Mandy and Mrs Smythe have noticed a definite improvement in their pupils' focus and attention on the task. The Head is pleased with the results and states that yes, 'titling your head to the side' does seem to work. However, she cautions, there can be all sorts of reasons for this: perhaps it is the teachers' enthusiasm, perhaps it is because the pupils believe it will work, or possibly it is just a novelty effect.

Thinking deeply

What other reasons could explain why 'tilting your head' in this case study seemed to improve attention and learning?

If something works, is it important to know *why* it works? If yes, why? If no, then why not?

Myth	Fact
Formal education should start as early as possible.	There is no convincing neuroscientific evidence to back this up; although the first three years are an important period for brain development, so is later childhood. Evidence has shown the surprising extent to which the brain is still developing in adolescence.
Certain food supplements can make you smarter.	Although the benefits of various food supplements have been well publicized, existing research suggests the most important nutritional issue to influence educational performance and achievement is having a good healthy diet, in particular the importance of having breakfast. Nowadays many schools have breakfast clubs and all schools promote healthy eating.
You can never drink enough water.	Scientific evidence states that even small amounts of dehydration can impair the ability to think and concentrate; as a result of these findings, drinking water has been promoted as a way to improve learning. However, recent research with adults has shown that drinking water when you are not thirsty can *impair* learning. Therefore, in schools children should be encouraged to drink water when thirsty. It should also be noted that in very hot weather, children's ability to be aware of when they are thirsty is less reliable, so in this situation children need to be encouraged to drink water even when they think they don't need to.
The amount of hours you sleep is *not* important.	Evidence suggests that sleep is important and that it helps us to lay down and consolidate what we have learnt. As well as helping us remember what we learned when we were awake, sleep also helps us prepare to learn more and use what we know to generate insights.

Myth	Fact
Specific exercises help the learning process.	All forms or exercise have advantages. Research has shown that the ability to focus and avoid distraction improves after 30 minutes of aerobic endurance exercise. It is recommended that physical education should be scheduled *before* lessons begin and particularly before demanding lessons, rather than being scheduled after the school day has finished.
You can learn without being aware that you are learning.	Implicit learning is said to happen when the brain absorbs information without being consciously aware that it is doing so. It would be nice to think that your brain is a sponge and that you just have to sit in class and that the information will just somehow soak into your mind. Research has found that there seems to be doubt as to whether implicit learning applies to tasks which relate to thinking. It does seem that additional activity occurs in our brain when we are learning something new, and that the more time we spend actively thinking, the more likely we are to remember the information.

Source: Hall 2005

Language and communication skills

The ability to communicate is essential to what is being human. But how do we communicate? Most of us communicate with a recognized language, be it English, French or Urdu. And even if we did not have language, we could still communicate through facial expressions and body language. Indeed many of us can tell stories of how we were on holiday in some location where we did not know the language but still we somehow managed to make ourselves understood.

Furthermore, there are individuals who are deaf and who perhaps use an alternative system such as British Sign Language. In addition, there are some individuals who, due to a combination of disabilities or impairments, might use systems such as communication boards or Makaton. (For further information on these systems, see Chapter 4.)

The point that is being made here is that there are many different ways of communicating and that spoken language is only one form of communication. All languages share certain common features. All languages use symbols. These symbols can be words, or they can be signs. The symbols themselves are arbitrary. For example, the word 'dog' looks and sounds nothing like what it represents and indeed different languages have different words that mean dog. What is important is that all speakers of the language understand these shared meanings. The next feature is that language is governed by rules such as word order. For example, we know that 'Timmy kisses Mummy' is not the same as 'Mummy kisses Timmy'. Finally there is a creative element to language which we can see in poetry and in the way that language changes and evolves over time.

The extent of an individual's language can be expressed in terms of receptive and expressive abilities. **Receptive language** describes how much an individual can understand, while **expressive language** outlines how much an individual can communicate. In the course of normal development, a child learning to speak will always understand more than they can say.

Stages of language acquisition

Early language development

Babies are born with the ability to discriminate, i.e. to hear the difference between all possible human speech sounds. This ability disappears well before the end of the first year, at which time the child will only be able to recognize those speech sounds which occur in their native language. From very early on, conversation skills are developed and practised. Psychologists have observed how mothers will talk to their young babies. In such conversations a mother will treat the baby as an equal participant (Snow 1977). Imagine the following:

Mother: You are a lovely baby. (Pauses.)
Baby: (Moving its arms while looking at mother.)
Mother: Is that right?

It is through such dialogues that conversation skills such as turn-taking begin to develop.

From about one month old the baby starts cooing (making vowel sounds). At five months the baby begins babbling (repeating one syllable over and over again). About this time and well before the baby utters its first words, the baby will use its eyes to communicate with people. A baby will follow their mother's eyes, catch her attention and then move their eyes to something which they want their mother to see. The ability to follow another person's gaze is called **gaze monitoring** and is essential to language development. For example, a mother might look at the bus and say: 'There's our bus.' Now if the baby is to eventually associate a bus with the word 'bus', then it is crucial that the baby follows their mother's gaze and looks at what their mother is looking at. If a child did not have this ability to follow another's gaze then language development would be affected. If the mother said, 'Look at the bus', and the child was looking at a lamp post then the child might think that the word 'bus' was associated with the *lamp post*. This could lead to the child calling lamp posts buses.

Babies will also use pointing. **Instrumental pointing** involves pointing at something that they want but that they can't get for themselves, e.g. the biscuit jar on the top shelf. **Proto-declarative pointing**, on the other hand, is pointing with the intention of sharing an experience; for example, when a baby points to a lady in a large hat as if to say: 'Just look at that hat!' At eleven to twelve months, babbling becomes more speech-like in form and has the same intonation and emphasis as adult speech. It is at this point that babies from different nationalities will sound different. The first words will appear around about twelve months.

Development of grammar

At about eighteen months the child is using **holophrases**. These are one-word sentences used in combination with gestures. For example, a child points at a chocolate biscuit and jumps up and down while saying 'biscuit'. The next stage has been described as **telegraphic speech**. At this stage the child will use only the key words. For example, if you ask a child from about twenty to twenty-four months to say 'I am eating a chocolate biscuit', then they will probably say, 'Eat biscuit.' As the child begins to use more words to create longer sentences, they begin to experiment with and understand the rules which determine how words should be put together to form meaningful sentences. One common occurrence is **over-regularization** or **over-generalization** of rules. For example, at some time around three years of age the child will learn that past tense is indicated by putting the sound 'ed' at the end of a verb, e.g. 'Dogs growl. Yesterday the dog growled at me.' However, English is a complicated language and there are many exceptions. Children between the ages of three and five will often make mistakes regarding the over-generalization of rules and say such things as 'I goed shopping for biscuits.'

Theories of language learning

It is important to note that children learn language in a social context.

Bruner (1983) talked of formats that are of **repetitive routines**, which allow children to break the code of language. Repetitive routines refer to daily events in a child's life such as getting ready to go out, mealtimes and having a bath.

Case study 1.6

The development of language

Baby: (pointing at the biscuit jar while jumping up and down): Biq! Biq! Biq!

Mother: Does my little boy want a biscuit? Here you go. Here is a nice biscuit, a nice biscuit. (Mother hands over the biscuit.)

Some months later

Toddler: (pointing at the biscuit jar while jumping up and down): Me biscuit!

Mother: You want a biscuit. What do we say? 'May I have a biscuit, please?'

Toddler: Biscuit now! Biscuit now!

Mother: What do we say? 'May I have a biscuit, please?'

Toddler: Biscuit please.

Mother: That's a good boy. Here's the biscuit.

Some time later

Child: Mum! Give me a biscuit!

Mother: Say it properly: 'May I have a biscuit, please?'

Child: May I have a biscuit, please?

Mother: That's a good boy. Here's two of your favourite chocolate chip biscuits. Now what do you say?

Case study 1.6 illustrates many points, one being that language develops within a social context. It is clear that the 'asking for a biscuit' activity was what Bruner (1983) referred to as a repetitive routine or format. It is interesting to note that the mother's language over time remained very much the same. Bruner would say that it is due to parents saying the same things in the same way in reference to the same activity, day in, day out, that children can begin to break the code of language. Other psychologists (Snow and Ferguson 1977; Schachter and Strage 1982) have talked about the style of language that is used with very young children. The term they use is **motherese**:

- Speakers of motherese will usually speak in a higher-pitch voice and at a slower pace.
- Sentences are shorter and usually grammatically correct.
- Sentences are grammatically simple.
- Repetition is used often.
- Vocabulary is concrete in that it refers to objects or people that are present.

Theories of language development

Learning theory of language development

What differed in case study 1.6 was what the mother expected of the child at different ages and what was consequently rewarded. Case study 1.6 illustrates the learning theory of language development, i.e. language is learned through imitation and reinforcement. At the start of the example the child can only say 'biq', but saying 'biq' is rewarded by receiving the chocolate biscuit. To begin with the mother is reinforcing appropriate sounds, but over time what she is reinforcing changes from sounds to meaningful words to grammatically correct sentences and finally to culturally accepted language norms with words such as please and thank you.

The principles of learning can explain some aspects of language development; however, they cannot adequately explain the creative nature of language. The learning approach cannot explain how children will sometimes say things that they have never heard.

Nativist theory of language development

Another approach to language, which can explain the creative nature of language, states that rather than being learned, language ability is pre-programmed into the mind and that language ability emerges slowly as the individual matures. Chomsky (1965) outlined what he referred to as a **language acquisition device**: we are born with 'something' within our brain that allows us to develop language. Children from this viewpoint are seen as grammar machines. This approach sees the language environment as important because it triggers the development of the language acquisition device. One assumption of this approach is that it is easier to learn a language before puberty than afterwards, and that the earlier an individual learns a language the easier it is. This view is termed the **critical period hypothesis**.

An interactional theory of language development

Nowadays many theorists state that the learning theory and the nativist theory of language development are both correct. In a sense, language development can best be explained by an interaction between a maturing individual and their learning experiences.

Bilingual acquisition

An interesting area of current research concerning language is the acquisition of two languages. Bilingual acquisition can be simultaneous, i.e. the child, from infancy, can learn two languages at the same time. An example of this would be where the father is French and the mother is English and the parents wish the child to learn both languages. Usually, when this is the case, parents teach the child two languages by using the 'one person-one language' rule, i.e. Dad will speak French to the child, while Mum speaks English. The second form of bilingualism is called sequential and this involves the child first learning one language and then at some later stage being introduced to a second language. An example of this would be an Italian child who is fluent only in Italian, moving to England at the age of five and having at that point to learn English.

Stages in simultaneous language acquisition (Watson 1995)

1. Words from both languages are learned by associating words with concepts. For example, a child may point to a dog and say 'dog – chien', i.e. say both the English and French words for dog. Sometimes these two words may be blended or combined in some form.
2. The child is learning to speak in both languages and increasingly realizes that there are two separate systems of communication, but will make mistakes in terms of grammatical structure. For example, they might attempt to combine the two or apply the grammatical rules from one language to the other. This phase may last for one to two years.
3. The child is now fluent in two languages. The child may have learned to rigidly associate one language with one person or context. For example, they only speak Italian on weekends when Grandma comes to stay.

Processes and stages in sequential language acquisition (Watson 1995)

This theory assumes that the child is fluent in their first language and uses this first language as a starting point from which to learn the second. It is helpful at this stage to think of our example of a five-year-old Italian boy who moves to England.

1. *Interactional phase.* As social relationships are central to children, children will first learn key phrases that help them to interact and play with other children. These key phrases would include 'Can I play?', 'My turn' and 'No'.
2. *Interference.* Here the child is using the rules of their first language and trying to apply them to the second language. This will result in errors.
3. *Silent period.* Some children will speak very little when they are first exposed to the second language. This phase can possibly last several months. It is thought that this phase allows the child to build up an understanding of what is being said around them. However, not all children go through this stage and the extent of this stage is thought to be determined by the child's learning style and personality.
4. *Code switching.* This is where the child switches from one language to the other in mid-stream, so to speak. This is quite normal and often children do this as they are imitating adults within their culture who are bilingual.
5. *Language loss.* This is where one language has replaced the other. In an extreme example, the child will be exposed to the new language but have no one to talk to in their first language and thus, while learning the second language, they lose some of their abilities in their first.

According to the critical period hypothesis, a child before puberty will find it easier to learn a second language than an adult because their brain is more flexible. It is thought that children who learn a second language will take from one to two years to achieve **basic interpersonal communication skills** (language first learned by toddlers and pre-schoolers) and five to seven years to acquire **cognitive academic language proficiency** (the language used within classroom contexts and the standard necessary to cope with GCSEs) (Cummins 1984; Collier 1995).

Case study 1.7

Language development

In Everytown Secondary, Jane (a cover supervisor) and Sian (a teaching assistant) were discussing aspects of language development with Colin (their Special education needs coordinator).

Jane: Well all this information on language development is interesting but it is very much geared to the early years.

Sian: How about expressive language and receptive language and that when children are learning a language they can always understand more than they can say? That equally applies to EAL [English as an additional language] pupils.

Jane: But what about turn-taking and repetitive routines, i.e. breaking the code of language by saying the same things in the same way in the same setting? OK, you do that with very young children but do you do that with secondary pupils?

Colin: The challenge with teaching any new information, including a language, is trying to apply the knowledge of learning to the age that you are working with. Now, Jane, you often cover maths classes – would you say that there is a specific vocabulary in maths?

Jane: Do you mean like quadratic equations?

Colin: And Sian, you are supporting the science classes. Is there specific terminology the pupils need to know?

Sian: Do you mean . . . like photosynthesis?

Colin: If your subject has specific terminology, then how do you help pupils learn this terminology? Do you use techniques of turn-taking and repetitive routines?

Thinking deeply

What subjects do you support?
  What are specific examples of terminology within your subject area?
  How do you help pupils to learn this terminology? (Refer to techniques such as turn-taking, repetitive routines, reinforcement, etc.)

Social and emotional skills

Psychologists have described people as social animals. Social interaction, being involved with others, is a vital element of most people's lives. Although we may be able to remember how we learned to read and write, most of us will find it difficult to say how we learned to interact with others. Social and emotional skills are not normally taught in school, but somewhere along the line most of us will have learned enough skills to get by. Most of us will be able to think of people who are very good at social skills. These individuals appear confident and relaxed in social gatherings and seem to be very good at knowing just the right thing to say. On the other hand we probably also know people who stand too close to others in lifts, who are extremely awkward and never say the right thing.

Theory of mind

Psychologists now believe that in order to fully engage in the social world we need to develop a theory of mind. A **theory of mind** involves the awareness that:

* As you have thoughts, emotions and feelings, so do other people.
* As your beliefs about the world influence your behaviour, other people's behaviour will be influenced by their beliefs.
* Different people will have different beliefs.
* By watching what a person does, you can to some extent guess what they are thinking and feeling.

Researchers (Baron-Cohen *et al.* 1985) investigated the concept of theory of mind by giving children what has become known as the Sally-Ann task. The task goes like this:

* Sally and Ann are both in the room.
* While Ann is watching Sally hides the marble under the basket.
* Sally leaves the room.
* Ann takes the marble from the basket and hides the marble under the box.
* Ann leaves.
* Sally returns.

The child is then asked: 'Where will Sally look for her marble?' We know that the marble is now hidden under the box because we saw Ann hide it there. But we also know that Sally *doesn't know what we know* because she did not see Ann take the marble from its original hiding place and hide it somewhere else. Therefore Sally is going to look for the marble in the place where she hid it. This kind of reasoning involves a theory of mind and this skill is developed by most children by the age of four.

However, some children with Autism Spectrum Conditions will struggle with this concept. (For further information on Autism Spectrum Conditions, see pages 105–8.)

The development of empathy

Empathy is an important social skill. Hoffman (1982) saw empathy as first matching or experiencing the same emotion as another person and that this heightened emotion would lead to an increased desire to help. Hoffman saw empathy developing in stages. The stages are:

1. *Global empathy.* This develops during the first year. At this stage the young child will match the emotions of the other person. For example, if a young child sees his mother crying, then he will cry too.
2. *Egocentric empathy.* This stage begins to develop from about twelve to eighteen months. Again the child responds to another's distress with distress of their own, but then goes on to offer comfort. However, what they offer as comfort tends to be what they themselves would find comforting. A young child who observes their mother crying because she has just caught her finger in the door might offer her their favourite teddy.

Figure 5 Empathy involves the ability to imagine what others are feeling.

3. *Empathy for another's feelings.* This stage begins at about two to three years of age. Here the child both recognizes and partially matches the emotion. For example, a four-year-old child will realize that their eighteen-month-old brother is upset and be upset themselves, but not to the same degree. Again the child will offer something as a comfort, but now will offer an appropriate item of comfort. In this case, the four-year-old will *not* give her eighteen-month-old brother her own favourite teddy, but will quickly search for her brother's blanket that he likes to chew. As children grow older, they become more able at recognizing a wider range of emotions.

4. *Empathy for another's life condition.* This stage begins in late childhood or adolescence, corresponding to Piaget's stage of formal operations. The child now has developed a more generalized view of others' feelings and can imagine how individuals might feel in certain situations, for example, what it is like for children growing up in countries that are afflicted with famine.

Although Hoffman has outlined stages in regard to empathy, perhaps the more interesting question relates to how children learn to express concern for others. Children learn how to be thoughtful and considerate by observing others being thoughtful and considerate. This is a clear example of observational learning. It is helpful to tell children to be thoughtful and considerate, but it is essential to do what you say. If there is a conflict between what you say and what you do, children will imitate what you do. This is an example of actions speaking louder than words.

Stages in friendship

Selman and Jaquette (1977) outlined stages in the understanding of friendship. You will notice that the age at which a child enters a stage will vary.

Hartup (1994) argues that the best childhood predictor of how we function as an adult is not school grades or classroom behaviour but the degree to which we get on with other children. Friendships according to Hartup (1994) are important as they provide:

* *Emotional resources.* Friendships give children and young people the security to explore new situations, can serve to alleviate stress from bullying and divorce, and of course are a source of fun, joy and laughter.
* *Cognitive resources.* Children can learn knowledge and problem-solving skills from each other. Theorists talk about the benefits that peer

tutoring, peer modelling, cooperative learning and peer assessment can provide.

- *Opportunities to learn social skills.* Within friendships children and young people learn how to share, negotiate, cooperate and resolve conflict.

Harris (1997) argues that although children need parents for care and protection, it is our social groups, i.e. our friendships and peer group, who make us who we are. Friends serve as important models and can help to keep us on the straight and narrow. However, common sense tells us that the influence of friendships can be a force for both good and bad – friends can also be seen as a negative influence with parents fearing that their child may get into the 'wrong crowd'. Indeed, Gosline (2008: 39) states that one type of teen criminal is drawn into crime by the 'glamorous allure of badass friends'.

Friends are important, and research has found that children and young people who have stable friendships on average have more positive attitudes to school and are less likely to be bullied (Fox and Boulton 2006). Furthermore, other researchers have found that a lack of stable friendships predicted lower levels of achievement and higher levels of emotional distress (Wentzel, Barry and Caldwell 2004) and that isolation from peers in childhood was linked with mental health issues in adulthood (Cowen *et al.* 1973; Bagwell *et al.* 1998).

Table 1.1 Stages in friendship

Age 3–7	*Momentary playmates.* A friend is someone who you play with.
Age 4–9	*One-way assistance.* A friend is someone who helps you. However, the idea that you help your friend has not been fully developed.
Age 6–12	*Fair weather cooperation.* A friendship involves helping each other out. However, friendships at this stage can be fragile as minor setbacks or conflicts can result in the breaking of the friendship.
Age 9–15	*Intimate friendship.* Involves intimacy, mutuality and will continue despite minor setbacks and conflicts.
Age 12+	*Autonomous interdependence.* Friendships involve intimacy and mutuality but friendships grow and change with time. A friend is not possessive but recognizes and accepts their own and their friend's need for other relationships.

It is important to realize that these studies are highlighting links and that they are not saying that difficulties in friendships *cause* later problems in life. There can be many reasons for not achieving in school and for having mental health issues in adulthood.

Further interesting research (Rubin and Coplan 1992) has looked at concepts of popularity and has identified children as being popular, average, controversial, rejected and neglected. Those children who were classified as neglected or rejected were seen to be in need of social skills training.

In summary, the research indicates that friendships are important and if a child or young person is experiencing problems with making and keeping

Table 1.2 Examples of school-related social skills

School expectations	• Use appropriate forms of seeking attention such as raising hands and waiting turns • Staying on task and trying your best even if you find the task difficult • Following directions • Being polite • Working independently
Interpersonal skills	• Being able to start and have conversations with others • Know appropriate greetings • Able to take turns • Can join in and is able to ask others to join in • Able to listen to others • Cooperates with others • Able to empathize with how others are feeling • Able to offer help • Can resolve conflicts with peers and reach compromises • Can accept compliments
Accepting negatives	• Can deal positively with mistakes • Accepts responsibility for own behaviour • Can appreciate and deal with the consequence of their own actions • Can understand and accept that 'no' means 'no'
Self-control and awareness	• Can understand and describe own feelings • Can appreciate the link between feelings and behaviour • Can control temper and impulsivity • Can cope with anger and frustration • Can deal with losing • Can reward and motivate oneself

Source: Adapted from Schoenfeld *et al.* 2008: 20

friends then this needs to be addressed. As the value of friendship has long been recognized, a search through the literature reveals many different types of interventions going back many years.

Furman *et al.* (1979) identified four- and five-year-old children who seldom played with other children. They arranged for these children to have special play sessions with younger children. It was hoped that through playing with younger children, play activities could be practised and that this would lead them to feel more confident in social interactions. This did seem to help. O'Connor (1972) worked with a group of junior school children that had been identified as shy and withdrawn. These children were shown a film of a shy, withdrawn pupil who gradually and slowly over time became increasingly better at relating to other children. It was hoped that the children would imitate what they had seen on the film and again this proved successful. Oden and Asher (1977) taught socially isolated eight- and nine-year-olds specific skills such as how to cooperate, communicate and participate with other children. These children were seen to improve on social interactions and these improvements could still be seen a year later.

More recently, social skills training has been incorporated into programmes such as Social and Emotional Aspects of Learning (SEAL). (For further information on SEAL, see pages 42–4.)

Lists of social skills, like those given in the table, can be used in many ways. Schoenfeld *et al.* (2008) suggest that once a pupil is seen to be in need of help, a desired skill to be developed is identified and then the pupil is either taught the skill or instructed in the appropriate use of the skill. In terms of taking an inclusive approach, it is important to recognize the pupil's role in this process and that they are actively encouraged to select a skill that they would like to work on.

Case study 1.8

Making friends is a skill

Georgia is a very bright child and she knows it; furthermore, she makes sure everyone else knows it. Georgia always speaks out of turn and has a habit of sniggering at other pupils' answers – and then she wonders why no one wants to play with her at break.

Greg, on the other hand, is so shy it is painful. He never looks at anyone and, for the most part, the other pupils don't even know that he is there.

It is obvious that both Greg and Sarah need help in making friends.

Thinking deeply

How would you apply the theory on friendships and social skills to both explain and determine ways forward for Greg and Georgia? Does the theory regarding friendships and social skills relate to any pupils you work with? If so, how?

Emotional intelligence

More recently psychologists have been interested in the topic of **emotional intelligence**. Emotional intelligence is more than being socially skilled, being a nice person or behaving well. For Goleman, an emotionally intelligent person is a person who:

- knows and manages their own feelings well
- reads and deals effectively with other people's feelings
- can motivate themselves and persist in the face of frustrations
- can control impulse and delay gratification
- can regulate their moods and keep distress from swamping their ability to think, and
- can empathize and hope (1996, in Pickard 1999: 55–6).

Goleman sees the goal as 'raising the level of social and emotional competence in children as part of their regular education – not just something taught remedially to children who are faltering and identified as "troubled," but a set of skills and understandings essential for every child' (1996: 262). Such programmes include components on self-awareness, personal decision making, managing feelings, handling stress, developing empathy, becoming a good communicator, self-disclosure, insight, self-acceptance, personal responsibility, assertiveness, group dynamics and conflict resolution.

Table 1.3 The six-step traffic light poster for teaching impulse control

Red light	1	Stop, calm down, and think before you act
Yellow light	2	Say the problem and how you feel
	3	Set a positive goal
	4	Think of lots of solutions
	5	Think ahead to the consequences
Green light	6	Go ahead and try the best plan

Source: Goleman 1996: 276

One example, which involves teaching impulse control to Year 5 pupils, involved a traffic light poster with six steps. Pupils were encouraged to go through these steps if they felt very angry and wanted to hit someone, or if they felt very upset and wanted to burst into tears. The steps are outlined in Table 1.3.

New directions in Social and Emotional Aspects of Learning (SEAL)

Most schools are now involved with programmes that focus on social and emotional aspects of learning. The rationale for such programmes is that if pupils are better able to understand themselves and others and are taught specific skills relating to empathy, self-awareness and managing distressing emotions, then they are more able to learn and are more likely to adopt positive behaviours. Many teaching professionals will state that pupils who are feeling anxious, upset or afraid are unlikely to be able to focus on the academic tasks required of them. Certainly such programmes relate to the *Every Child Matters* agenda (ECM).

Specific programmes, such as SEAL, aim to develop self-awareness, skills in managing one's feelings, motivation, empathy and other social skills. In primary school, the materials are organized under themes to include: new beginnings, getting on and falling out, saying no to bullying, going for goals, good to be me, and relationships and changes. Evaluations of SEAL programmes in primary schools (Hallam 2009) suggest that such programmes give pupils a vocabulary to talk about their emotions and that they have given staff greater knowledge and specific strategies for dealing with behaviour and emotional issues.

However, it is a sad fact that there are some pupils who have suffered unimaginable trauma in their short lives and that these pupils will require additional intensive and professional interventions.

Related to social and emotional aspects of learning is the concept of well-being and happiness. Layard (Institute for the Future of the Mind 2007) starts with the assumption that the aim of education should be to help pupils lead happy lives and that a discussion is needed regarding how to help pupils to achieve this. Furthermore, Layard (ibid: 5) states that research from psychology has shown that people who care more about others are in fact happier individuals; but that you can't make people happier by just telling them to care more. Likewise, people who constantly compare themselves with others are less happy; but telling pupils not to compare themselves does not necessarily mean that pupils will stop doing this. This statement has implications for programmes targeting social and emotional aspects of learning and well-being. In such programmes, factual information needs to be presented, but for factual information to make a difference pupils need to be actively involved in the learning. Thus, saying to a pupil that in order to be happy you need to care about others is not enough – the pupil has to discover this for themselves. The role of those involved in such programmes is to facilitate this process.

Case study 1.9

Helping a student to change

Real change needs to be self-directed. The role of those supporting teaching and learning is to enable pupils to 'get it' for themselves.

Maria (TA):   Why do you think you were sent out of the class?
Leona: Don't know.
Maria (TA):   Your teacher said you were arguing with the other girls in your group.
Leona: They all have it in for me.
Maria (TA):   Well, what started the argument?
Leona: They started it!
Maria (TA):   Well, what did you say?
Leona: Can't remember.

Several months later after PHSE (Personal, Health and Social Education) classes

Maria (TA):   Leona you really seem to be getting on with the others in your class.
Leona: Those classes really did change me. One of the lessons, it was the lesson you know how other people see you. And when you bitch about someone to someone else, how they are thinking that you could be doing this to them.
Maria (TA):   How did that make you feel?
Leona: I do that sometimes and when I am stressed or pissed off or someone is really annoying me I bitch about them to someone else. But the lesson really made me think.
Maria (TA):   What did you think?
Leona: Maybe that was why others don't like me. I thought: 'You know what? I don't want to be a mean person'.
Maria (TA):   So what do you do now?
Leona: I try to say to myself that being mean is not someone who I want to be and then I try not to say it.

Source: adapted from Britton 2008

Case study 1.10

An experiential lesson plan

Aim: To become more aware of friendships and how friendships can be made, broken and repaired.
Tasks:

- Create a picture with plasticene about how it feels to have a good friendship.
- Create a picture with plasticene of how it feels to fall out with your friend.
- Create a picture with plasticene of how it feels to make up with your friend.
- Discuss in pairs your pictures and then share your thoughts and pictures with the larger group.

Note: Pupils will be given 5 minutes to do each picture. While they are doing each picture, appropriate music will be played.

Thinking deeply

Within the lesson described in case study 1.10, how are pupils being actively encouraged to think about friendship?

What examples have you seen where pupils have been actively encouraged to think about social and emotional aspects of learning?

How successful have these approaches been?

Moral development

Headlines which focus on 'feral children' and 'escalating incidences of aggression within the classroom' could be seen as just another moral panic. On the other hand, perhaps such incidences of 'out-of-control' pupils highlight the need to look at moral development and, specifically, the role that adults play in fostering goodness and positive behaviour.

Morality can be defined as an internal sense of what is right or wrong. In considering what it is to be moral, attention has been focused on emotional, behavioural and cognitive components. A 'moral person' has the ability to empathize with another person's distress and feels guilt when they cause distress or harm. A moral person will engage in pro-social behaviours such as helping and sharing. Further, a moral person has the ability to reason and think about moral issues and understands why moral behaviour

Figure 6 Staff and pupils' pictures of various emotions were amazingly similar.

is important for society. Many psychologists have focused on how these emotions, thinking processes and behaviours develop over time; hence the term moral development.

While theories relating to moral development are interesting, what those involved in the teaching profession would like to know is how to instil a sense of right or wrong, how to encourage pro-social behaviour and how to foster goodness. Again we come to strategies based on social learning theory and behaviourism. Social learning theory would advocate modelling, that those involved in teaching demonstrate the behaviours they wish others to copy. Theories of behaviourism would argue that acts of kindness should be rewarded, while theories of induction would encourage children to think about moral issues in an atmosphere that is supportive and nurturing for the child. Moral discussions should be set at a level slightly above the child's stage of thinking. Again this relates to concepts of scaffolding and working within a child's Zone of Proximal Development. Part of this moral discussion would involve discussing with the child the consequences of their actions. Discussions relating to relevant moral issues might occur within PHSE (Personal Social and Health Education) classes, Circle Time, SEAL programmes or classes involved in encouraging personal, learning and thinking skills.

Table 1.4 Milestones in moral and pro-social development

Age	Abilities	Examples	Implications for support staff
1–2 years	A young child becomes aware of another's distress and will offer comfort.	If a child sees that a younger child is upset they may go up to them and give them a hug.	Those involved in early years can build on a child's natural potential for offering comfort and helping others by praising such behaviour.
3–6 years	While a child might start showing signs of guilt for bad behaviour by the age of 3, Freud believes the conscience to be developed by the age of 5 or 6. The conscience is thought to be the internalization of the punishing parent and it is your conscience that punishes you when you feel you have done something wrong. Freud would argue that it is feelings of guilt that prevents individuals from behaving badly.	A child of 5 who has deliberately broken another child's toy may feel guilty.	According to Freud, feelings of guilt are a sign that an individual knows that they have done something wrong. Feeling guilty is unpleasant and teaching staff may need to help children make amends for their wrongdoings.

Age	Abilities	Examples	Implications for support staff
5–9 years	In terms of moral reasoning, Piaget would argue that young children see rules as sacred and that actions are judged on consequences rather than intentions. Furthermore, at this stage children's behaviour is motivated by what others think and children behave to gain rewards or avoid punishment.	If a girl broke her sister's toy, even if it was an accident, a child at this stage would believe that the girl should be punished. Consequences are more important than intentions.	Thinking about why something is wrong or right is important and this skill needs to be encouraged.
10–16 years	Thinking about issues of morality becomes more developed. Children and young adults realize that intentions are more important than consequences, and begin to understand the concept of society and what is needed for society to operate.	If a girl broke her sister's toy by accident then a child or young adult at this stage would believe that the girl should not be punished as intentions should be taken into consideration.	Encouraging pupils to think about intentions and consequences is key.

Case study 1.11

Restorative justice

Restorative justice, originally a technique used in the criminal justice system, is now being used in many schools to resolve conflicts. Restorative justice aims to restore relationships between individuals where the relationships have broken down due to inappropriate or offending behaviour.

As Lee, a TA in a large secondary school, comments:

> When I arrived at the school I was warned by other members of staff to be careful of where I parked. I soon realized the importance of this when, to my horror, I found my front windscreen had been smashed by a bottle that had been thrown out of a second-storey window by a pupil whom I supported. I was shocked, upset and extremely angry, and I did not think it right that I should continue to support this pupil. When restorative justice was suggested, a friend of mine stated that this was an easy opt-out and all the pupil had to give was a glib apology and then they would get away with the behaviour.
>
> However, I was impressed with the meeting. At first the pupil said that he did not know what all the fuss was about because my car was insured. But I had the opportunity to tell the pupil how I felt and how upset I was by what had happened. It's funny but I think that through listening to me, the pupil suddenly realized the impact his actions had had. The pupil said he was really sorry and agreed that he would personally pay the damages and would wash my car every week for a term as a way of making up for what he had done. Having this meeting with the pupil and the mediator who helped us to talk about these issues has really made a difference to my relationship with the pupil. From the pupil's point of view, I think it allowed him to make amends and to really understand why his behaviour was unacceptable. His attitude is so much more positive now. I don't think he would have learned this if he was just given a punishment.

Thinking deeply

What strategies for resolving conflicts does your school have?

In case study 1.11, how would theories of moral development explain the pupil's change of attitude?

Specific skills and abilities

Creativity

Creativity is a word that is used often but is a word that proves difficult to define. Various definitions of creativity have focused on the use of imagination, the ability to come up with novel and original solutions to problems and that the outcome of the creative process is a product of worth and value. In everyday conversation, when we talk about creative genius we might mention famous artists, inventors or scientists. While some definitions of creativity propose that to be creative involves making an outstanding contribution to society, other definitions claim that everyone has creative potential and is capable of creative expression. However, for individuals to fulfil their creative potential, creativity needs to be nurtured. This view of creativity has implications for all those involved in education because one of the aims of education should be to foster pupils' creative thinking. The challenge for those involved in teaching is how to do this. Mellou (1996) argued that creativity can be nurtured through creative environments, creative programmes and creative ways of teaching. Perhaps in discussing how to foster creative thinking, it is more useful to focus on the creative process rather than the creative product. The creative process involves having good

Figure 7 'Oh where – oh where have I put that original idea – oh where – oh where – can it be?'

ideas, thinking original thoughts, being good at problem solving, combining different bits of existing knowledge to create new ideas, thinking outside the box and transferring existing knowledge to new situations. It is clear that the skills involved in this are of value to society, but how do you come up with new ideas and how do you teach your pupils to do this?

In a sense the devil is in the detail. What do creative environments, programmes and ways of teaching look like? First let us look at transferring knowledge to new situations. Pupils find this difficult, as the following case study illustrates.

Case study 1.12

Bar diagram – what bar diagram?

Mandy was working with a group of year 9 pupils helping them to write up a short science investigation. The teacher has asked them to show their results using a bar diagram and this is when the trouble began.

Jim:	I can't do this!
Shona:	I don't know how to do this!
Mandy (TA):	You do bar diagrams in maths.
Shona:	Miss, this is science – not maths!
Mandy (TA):	But there is maths in science!
Jim:	But this is a science, and science is different.
Mandy (TA):	Science and maths are connected; you can use what you know in maths to help you in science. If I asked your maths teacher if you could do a bar diagram – what would he say?
Shona:	Oh – we can do it.

In case study 1.12, the teaching assistant needed to specifically remind the pupils that what they had learnt in one learning situation could be used in another leaning situation. This skill of applying existing knowledge to different situations is part of the creative process.

Table 1.5 How to encourage creativity

Strategy	Benefits
Provide choices in activities.	This encourages pupils to think about what they are doing.
Accept different ideas.	One TA commented that: 'often to encourage discussion, I tell the pupil that there are no right or wrong answers; it is whatever you think it is. This attitude encourages the shy or less confident pupil to contribute'.
Ask open-ended questions.	In open-ended questions there are no right or wrong answers, only different possibilities.
Praise all responses, including unexpected answers, irrelevant answers and answers that are clearly wrong. However, praise needs to be genuine and pupils need to see the connection between giving answers and engaging in thinking.	The fact that pupils are answering questions needs to be encouraged. What seems like irrelevant answers can be connected to relevant points. (For further information on prompts and probes, see pages 78–80.) Praising all responses boosts self-esteem and helps the pupils to feel safe and confident to take chances. Pupils need to feel safe to make mistakes because making mistakes is an important part of the learning process. Responding to pupil mistakes by saying: 'Great, now you can start learning!' can help pupils see mistakes in a more positive manner.
Model creative thinking and behaviour.	This is difficult – see case study 1.13

Case study 1.13

Modelling creative thinking

Sam was interested in creativity but realized that some of the pupils she worked with found problem solving and coming up with new ideas extremely difficult. They did not like being given choices: they wanted to be told what to do and they wanted to know what the 'right' answer was. Sam was working in a Year 6 class encouraging pupils to respond to a recent newspaper headline that said 'Due to new technologies the average life expectancy will soon be a hundred'. The teacher had asked the pupils to get into groups and to think about the possible consequences of this scientific breakthrough. Sam knew she had her work cut out in encouraging her group to think.

Karl:	People don't live to be a hundred.
Shona:	My grandma is eighty and she is ancient. She is always forgetting things.
Jordan:	My grandad is 75 and he is in a home; he can't walk any more.
Sam (TA):	Well, let us just imagine that people could live longer and that even at eighty or ninety-five they would be healthy and that they could think and remember things like you or me.
Jordan:	But that's not the way it is.
Sam (TA):	But let's just imagine it was possible. What would it mean?
Karl:	I don't know.
Jordan:	How are we supposed to know? It hasn't happened?
Sam (TA):	Let's just imagine. Now, if I was asked this question, I would think: 'Well, how would this affect me?'
Shona:	I don't get this!
Sam (TA):	I would think about something I do know about – for example, like going to work. Well for me, I'm due to retire at age 65.
Karl:	I didn't know that you were that old!
Sam (TA):	I'm not but if I did retire in my sixties, then I would have another forty years of not working.
Shona:	That would be great – you could do all sorts of things!
Karl:	I get it . . . but would the government want to pay pensions to people for forty years?
Jordan:	Yeah – what about getting married? If you get married to someone at twenty, are you promising to be with them forever!!!
Sam (TA):	Those are very good comments!

Sam later reported to the teacher about how she tried to model thinking about new ideas. As Sam said, 'It was not simply getting them to do what I do, but getting them to try and think how I think – and that is much harder!'

Thinking deeply

How do you try to model creative thinking?

Development of reading

Although we may not be able to remember how we learned to talk, most people will have vivid memories of learning to read and write. We may remember with some fondness our earliest readers, be they about 'Biff and Chip' or 'Janet and John'. We may remember how we learned to hold a pencil and how we felt when we had mastered joined-up writing. Much of the early school years focuses on literacy, which encompasses both reading and writing skills. Reading has been defined as the ability to extract meaning from the text. The skill of writing, while being related to reading, involves the fine motor skills involved in putting pen to paper and the ability to spell. In English, spelling is perceived by many as more difficult than reading, and on average there is about a year's gap between learning to read new words and learning to spell these words.

Reading is said to involve both **top-down** and **bottom-up processing**. Top-down processing refers to our knowledge of the world, including our knowledge of our spoken language, and how we use this knowledge to guide us in our understanding of the text. Imagine that a young child of five is asked to read the following: 'The duck said quack.' Now the child recognizes the words *'the'*, *'duck'* and *'said'*, but not the last word; she has never seen *'quack'* written. However, from the child's understanding of the world and her knowledge of language, she knows that ducks say 'quack'. Thus the child is able, from the context, to guess the last word. Here the child is using top-down processing to help her read the text.

Bottom-up processing, on the other hand, states that we create meaning by recognizing first the letters that make up the words, then the sound combinations that these letters make, and then finally we put these sound combinations together as words. Imagine a child of seven is asked to read the following: 'The witch raised her wand and said: "Olly-olly-tri-ma-golly".' If the child is to successfully read the witch's spell, then they will need to know the rules which state that certain letter combinations correspond to certain sounds. This example illustrates both bottom-up processing and **grapheme–phoneme awareness**.

Often children who have difficulty in learning to read are said to have poor grapheme–phoneme awareness. **Graphemes** can be defined as the letters of the alphabet. The letters of the alphabet alone, or in combination, correspond to particular **phonemes** or sound units. For example, the word *'cat'* is made up of three phonemes, *'kuh-aah-tuh'*, and these sound units or phonemes correspond to the letters or graphemes of *'c'*, *'a'* and *'t'*. Children who have difficulty in recognizing the link between letters and sounds will find reading and spelling difficult.

The English language is a difficult language to learn to read and spell for a number of reasons. To begin with, a child learning to read will have to come to grips with the twenty-six letters of the alphabet and the forty-four sound combinations that these letters can make. Furthermore, Bailey (1967) states that there are about 200 rules for combining sounds. For example, the two-vowel rule states that the first vowel says its name while the second is silent. However, there are always exceptions to the rules. So, while the rule holds true for words such as '*tie*' and '*eat*' it does not work for a word such as '*field*'.

Frith (1985) sees reading developing through the following three stages:

- *Logographic*, age 3–5. In this phase the child responds to text on a sight recognition basis. A young child of three might recognize the signs for Tesco or McDonald's. Here the child is not reading the individual letters but is responding to the particular visual pattern that the word makes. The 'look and say' method utilizes this strategy for reading. However, this approach has its limitations as children will often make mistakes between visually similar words such as '*black*' and '*block*'.
- *Alphabetic*, age 5–7. This stage involves the child developing a phonological awareness, i.e. an awareness that certain letters correspond to certain sounds. With a knowledge of phonics, a beginning reader can start to sound out unfamiliar words.
- *Orthographic*, age 7–9+. This stage involves the child recognizing words by sight as distinctive letter combinations. The child does not have to sound out the word; the child recognizes the unique letter combinations that identify the word.

Concentration, attention and memory

Questions to start you thinking about memory

Do you think about how you remember information?
Do you think about why you forget information?
How do you think your memory works?
Can you control how well your memory works?
Do you think you have a good memory?
What things are you good at remembering?
What things do you find difficult to remember?
Do you have specific strategies that you use to remember information?
What are these strategies? Are some of your strategies more successful than others?

Have you ever been in a situation where you meet someone you know but you have forgotten their name? If yes, then how do you try to remember their name without asking them? Have you ever been in a situation where you know that you know the answer but you can't remember it? If yes, then do you have a specific strategy for trying to remember this information? Do you think that thinking about your memory is helpful? How? Do you think that helping pupils to think about how they remember would be useful? Why?

It is generally believed that a child's ability to concentrate, pay attention and remember is poorer than that of an adult and that these abilities develop with age. Certainly young children have difficulties remembering their telephone number and address, and young children are limited in the time that they can actually sit and listen to the teacher. However, in saying that, young children can memorize and retell their favourite story and even the most fidgety pupil can often sit and play a video game for hours. It seems that memory for some events is easier than others. When an event is personally interesting or meaningful, then we are not aware that we are remembering – memory just happens. However, when we are asked to remember an item which is not personally meaningful, the act of remembering needs to be conscious and deliberate.

The skills of concentration, attention and memory are interrelated. For example, let us imagine a Year 2 pupil who is trying to learn a list of spelling words for a test on Friday. To learn the words:

1. The child must pay *attention*, i.e. the child must focus on those specific words.
2. Then the child must *concentrate*, i.e. the child must focus on those words, specifically the individual letters that make up those words.
3. Finally the child must *remember* this information, i.e. the child must commit the information to memory.

When we talk about the processes involved in remembering we are talking about memory. Memory involves three stages: **encoding, storage** and **retrieval**. First the individuals must encode the information to be learned. Information can be encoded either verbatim, i.e. word for word, or the gist of the event can be stored. How the information is to be encoded depends on the task. For example, if a list of spelling words is to be remembered, then the memory has to be letter for letter. However, if you were asked to remember what happened in a film, then you would not remember the film word for word; instead, you would remember the gist of the film, i.e. the essence or key points. Once information is encoded it is stored. According to Piaget, information will be stored in the form of schemas. (For further information on schemas, see pages 12–14.) Once information is stored then it can be retrieved later or recollected when needed.

Memory has also been thought of as being divided into short-term memory, working memory and long-term memory. (For further information on working memory, see pages 144–5.) Short-term and working memory consist of everything we are currently thinking about at any one point in time, whereas long-term memory is where we store information. Information in long-term memory is transferred into our working memory when the need arises.

It has been found that the capacity of short-term memory, i.e. the amount of information that we can hold in our short-term memory, increases over the years until as adults we can hold seven (plus or minus two) units of information. Asking a person to immediately recall a string of random digits (e.g. 8 4 5 2 9 6 1 3) tests this capacity. Research has revealed that as children become older, they realize that in order to remember unrelated information (for example, how to spell dinosaur, or recall their times tables) they must do something special with this information. This something special is referred to as a **memory strategy**. Ornstein *et al.* (1975) compared strategies used by Year 3 and Year 8 pupils when asked to remember a list of words that the teacher read out loud to them. The teacher would read a list of words (such as cow, table, cup, tree and car). The pupils were asked to repeat the words out loud as they heard them. This is what the younger pupils did. However, while saying the new word, the older pupils would also take the time to rehearse the previous words. Miller (1990) noted differences in approaches to homework. Year 8 pupils were better at selecting relevant material and ignoring irrelevant material than younger pupils. It also seems that to remember unrelated information, it is important not only that the information is stored but also that the information is organized because organization improves recall.

It would be nice to think that all information taught at school was personally meaningful and that memory would just happen. Part of the reason behind a child being actively involved in the learning process is to create learning situations that are meaningful. However, the reality is that most pupils at some point will struggle to remember what is taught. Much research has focused on **metamemory**, i.e. the knowledge someone has of their own memory processes. In terms of encouraging children to remember what is being taught in school, children need to realize that they need to put an effort into remembering, and that remembering unrelated information requires memory strategies. Children need to be aware of what strategy they are using and to monitor whether the strategy is working or not. Furthermore, if the strategy is not working then the children need to be able to find another strategy.

Recent attention on metamemory has focused on the importance of self-awareness and self-control (Dehn 2008).

Self-awareness involves:

- knowing your own skills and cognitive abilities; for example, knowing what strategies you employ to learn
- being able to understand how your own skills and abilities match up to the task at hand
- knowing what processes and strategies will enable you to successfully complete a task.

Self-control involves being consciously aware and able to:

- select and use appropriate strategies
- monitor, manage, control and evaluate how you are using these strategies.

Obviously these are quite complex skills.

Case study 1.14

Being self-aware

Jason was revising for his biology exam. He was looking at past exam papers. He came to a section on photosynthesis. Jason realized that he had always scored badly on photosynthesis questions in practice tests in class. Jason looked at his past test papers and realized that when it came to the test he always got the key terms muddled up. Jason then realized that he needed to find a way to learn these key terms. At this point Jason tried to think about how he learned and remembered best. After some thought, Jason realized that he remembered best through pictures and stories – so he then set out to draw a picture and create a story about photosynthesis. The next day, when Jason was once again revising, he decided to test himself on how much he remembered about photosynthesis. He was pleased that, by remembering his story, he could now remember most of the key concepts of photosynthesis. However, Jason was still confusing two concepts: 'chloroplasts' with 'chlorophyll'. His notes stated, 'Photosynthesis takes place in chloroplasts which have chlorophyll in them', so Jason decided to go back to his story and make that part more vivid and memorable. This is what he wrote: 'The intrepid explorer went to the place, the *plasticene* palace known as *Chloroplasts*, that was *filled* with little green machines called *chlorophyll*.' The next day when Jason came to revising, he realized that now he had photosynthesis nailed.

Thinking deeply

In case study 1.14, what evidence is there that Jason has both a self-awareness and self-control in regard to understanding how he learns and remembers? (In your answer, use terms such as monitoring and evaluating, etc.)

To what extent can you and do you encourage these skills in the pupils you work with?

Mathematical skills

Much time is spent on teaching children maths. But first it is helpful to define what we mean by maths. Bell *et al.* (1983) believed that teaching maths involved the learning of facts, skills, concepts, strategies, attitudes and, finally, an appreciation of maths. These were defined as:

- *Facts.* Mathematical facts include:
  - — Abbreviations, e.g. cm for centimetres.
  - — Conventions, e.g. $6x$ means six times x.
  - — Conversion factors, e.g. 32° Fahrenheit = 0° Celsius.
  - — Concepts, e.g. even numbers.
  - — Factual results, e.g. results of times tables.

- *Skills.* Skills are defined as a set of multi-step procedures that can be used in certain specific situations. For example, if a pupil is given the question $1/2 + 1/4$, a pupil who is competent in maths would realize that the first step in solving the problem is to find a common denominator for the fractions: $1/2 + 1/4 = 2/4 + 1/4 = 3/4$.
- *Concepts.* A concept refers to a property of an object. For example, all negative numbers are numbers less than zero.
- *General strategies.* A general strategy refers to ways of approaching a problem. A general strategy can be applied to many different types of problem. For example, when a pupil is asked to add $16 + 14$ in their head, the pupil might simplify the problem: $16 + 14 = 10 + 10 + 6 + 4 = 30$. Simplification is a general strategy.

- *Attitudes.* Attitudes refers to a person's feelings and emotional responses. It is hoped that pupils come to enjoy and feel confident about maths.
- *Appreciation.* An appreciation of maths involves the pupil realizing the usefulness of maths in society and everyday life.

It is the aim of the National Curriculum to specifically teach strategies that relate to using, communicating and developing ideas of argument or proof in mathematics. Mathematical skills, like many skills, build on previously learned knowledge. It is hoped that the way in which maths is taught will develop positive attitudes and an appreciation of maths. What is first taught in schools lays the foundation for what is taught later. A pupil must master the initial concepts before they can move on and understand later concepts. For example, if a child does not understand what is meant by 'more than' or 'less than', then the child will not be able to say whether 17 is more than 15. Piaget's views on learning as an interaction between the child being actively involved with his environment and maturation are central to maths teaching. Maturation limits what can be taught at certain ages. Piaget's views on the development of logic have influenced when mathematical concepts are introduced. For example, could you teach a child of four their times tables? Possibly a four-year-old could memorize 'four times four is sixteen' – but would they really understand what is meant by multiplication? Real learning involves more than receiving and repeating back the knowledge parrot-fashion. Real learning involves making sense of the knowledge. Psychologists have described this process as constructing knowledge. Vygotsky's views on how knowledge is learned through social interaction is also central to mathematical teaching, because children learn about maths by talking about how to do maths problems, i.e. what strategies to use, with a more experienced person.

Thinking deeply

Do you agree or disagree with the following statements?

Individuals either have a mathematical ability or they don't.
Individuals who are good at maths are really smart.
Mathematical ability is something you are born with.
If you do not find maths easy then no amount of practice will help.
Men and boys are naturally better at maths.
Being hopeless at maths is socially acceptable.

What is your attitude to mathematics?

Eastaway and Askew, in their 2010 book *Maths for Mums and Dads*, strongly recommend that parents should not tell their children that they are themselves hopeless at maths and, importantly, they should not revel or brag about the fact that they find maths difficult. This advice is based on Bandura's ideas (see pages 24–5 and 82) that children learn about expectations and self-concepts through modelling and reinforcement. Imagine if a parent who hears that their child has failed a maths exam says, 'Never mind – I always failed my maths exams.' Now, on one level, this comment might make the child feel better – but it could also result in the child believing that it is alright not to be good at maths, or that maybe their poor result is because they are genetically tuned to be weak at maths and nothing they can do will make any difference. The implication of Eastaway and Askew's advice is that all those who support teaching and learning need to carefully consider how they respond to pupils who find maths difficult.

Thinking deeply

How would you respond to the following situation?

I was circulating around the class offering help and support to all those pupils who needed help with their maths worksheet. As I got to Amy I realized that she was not doing her maths worksheet but had taken out her reading book. When I asked her what she was doing, she replied: 'Oh, maths isn't really my thing; never has been.'

The development of fine and gross motor skills

Learning to physically move (e.g. crawl, walk, skip, hold a pencil, juggle) involves both **biological maturation** and interaction in the environment. For example, at a certain age we might develop the coordination to learn to skip but practice at skipping makes us better. To see an example of this, one only has to watch Year 2 boys and girls competing in a skipping race. Learning a physical skill involves both learning the sequence of actions that make up a skill and how to combine the sequence such that the movement appears graceful. Physical movements can involve the whole body, e.g. jumping **(gross motor skills)** or more refined movements using only certain body parts, e.g. handwriting **(fine motor skills)**. To organize physical movement, an individual is dependent upon the body receiving sensory information from the environment. Sensory information is received by **tactile receptors**, the **vestibular apparatus** and the **proprioceptive system** (Ripley *et al.* 1997). These are defined as:

- *Tactile receptors* are specialized cells within the skin that send the brain information about light, touch, pain, temperature and pressure.
- *Vestibular receptors* are located within the inner ear and automatically coordinate movements of the eyes, head and body in order to maintain balance.
- *Proprioceptors* are present in the muscles and joints and enable an individual to move their arms and legs without visual guidance. For example, we can do up the buttons on our coat without looking.

Any difficulties with processing sensory information could lead to problems with movement. In looking at this area, psychologists have developed a series of developmental milestones indicating what most children should be able to do at a certain age. Again it is important to stress that there will be individual variation. However, when a child is considerably delayed in reaching their developmental milestones, this could indicate conditions such as dyspraxia. (For further information on dyspraxia and other conditions, see Chapter 4.) Some examples of developmental motor milestones would be:

- *Five months.* Infant can transfer one object from hand to hand.
- *One year.* Infant pulls themselves up to stand; walks around furniture.
- *Eighteen months.* Toddler begins to show a preference for one hand; can throw and kick a ball without falling over.
- *Two and a half years.* Toddler can remove or unfasten coat; can put on simple items such as vest and pants.
- *Three and a half years.* Child can walk on tiptoes; can button up clothing; can draw a person that includes head, eyes, nose, mouth and legs.
- *Six years.* Child can hop and skip.

A full description of motor milestones can be found in Ripley *et al.* (1997: 29–33, 41–2).

Stages in handwriting

Ripley *et al.* (1997) outlined three stages in the development of handwriting.

Early phase

- Establishing a support hand and a dominant hand. The dominant hand needs to practise the specialized movements that correspond to letters.

The support hand needs to learn to move and hold the paper in position.

- Mastering the thumb-and-two-finger grip for holding pencils or pens.
- Learning the basic movement patterns corresponding to letters and numbers (because skilled writing involves fine finger and wrist movements).
- Mastering pencil control and maintaining appropriate pressure on the paper.

Middle phase

- Learning to maintain an even letter size and to place the letters on a line.
- Being able to use a variety of writing tools.

Final phase

- Speeding up of writing. Dutton (1989) reports that at the age of five a child can write up to one and a half words per minute, and this progresses to an average of eighteen words per minute at the age of sixteen.

In England it is customary that children beginning school first learn to print. Joined-up writing, or cursive script, is introduced at about age seven.

Summary

This chapter has covered numerous principles underlying pupil development and learning to include theories of cognitive development (Piaget), views regarding how language and communication skills are acquired, moral development, creativity and specific skills involved in reading and writing. Researchers (Blatchford *et al.* 2009) talk of the wider pedagogical role of support staff. This role encompasses all that TAs know about subject knowledge, child development and basic principles underlying pupil development and learning. Most importantly, it is also how TAs use this knowledge in their day-to-day, face-to-face interactions with pupils. Some pupils may have one specific need such as challenges in writing, but pupils come in all shapes and sizes, and with a combination of gifts, strengths and needs.

Thinking deeply

What combinations of gifts, strengths and needs do the pupils you support have?

How do you use your pedagogical knowledge, i.e. your knowledge of basic principles underlying pupil development and learning, to support the pupils you work with on a day-to-day basis?

Chapter 2

Learning support strategies

Learning strategies as a way to promote effective learning

From our own experience as both learners and people who work within classrooms, we know that there are many different ways of teaching. A teacher will know and use a variety of methods to support learning. For example, how were you taught your times tables? Did you have to stand up with your class and recite your times tables? Were you taught your times tables as a class or did you work your way through maths cards? How are children today taught their times tables? The art of teaching or supporting learning is about knowing a variety of methods and, more importantly, knowing when to use them. In this chapter, when we talk about ways or methods of teaching, we will be talking about learning support strategies. It is the aim of this chapter to outline a variety of learning support strategies.

To set the scene we are going to look at nine case studies. These nine case studies, along with some case studies referred to in Chapter 1, will be used to explore a variety of learning support strategies. As a teaching assistant you will be working under the direction of the teacher, and she or he will be designing many of the strategies outlined in this chapter. However, as a teaching assistant, you might be asked to help the teacher carry out these strategies on a day-to-day basis. By understanding how and why these strategies work, you will be in a better position to support the teacher and, moreover, be more able to effectively implement these strategies yourself when you are supporting pupils, individually or in groups.

Case study 2.1

An idea for learning about weight

Sarah, a teaching assistant, was working with a group of Year 1 children. Sarah had chosen five classroom objects and wrapped them in brightly coloured paper and covered them with bows. The children were very excited when they saw the packages. The children jumped up and down and kept asking whose birthday it was and when they could open the presents. Sarah explained to the children that they were going to play a game about weight. To play the game they had to decide which package was the heaviest. Sarah had each child in turn pick up the packages and give their ideas on which package was the heaviest and which was the lightest. The children took turns to weigh one parcel each. Each child would place the package on one side of the scale and use multi-link pieces to balance the scales. The children had to count and record how many multi-link pieces were needed to balance the scales.

Case study 2.2

Difficulty with essays

Donna, a teaching assistant, was working in a Year 9 English class. The teacher talked about advertisements and how they are an example of persuasive speech. The pupils were given a handout that contained two advertisements regarding the merits of Tenerife. The pupils were asked to write a short essay comparing the differences between the advertisements in terms of form, purpose, audience, content, language and presentation. The teacher added that this essay would contain an introduction, a middle bit with facts, and an ending with their own thoughts and conclusions. Donna was working with a small group of pupils who found it difficult to write essays. Although the teacher had outlined the structure of an essay, these pupils struggled and seemed not to know where to begin.

Discovery/active learning

Piaget would describe the lesson on weight as an example of **discovery learning**. Piaget believed that individuals had to be actively involved in the learning process. Imagine you were trying to teach a child about weight. You could, in order to teach the concept of weight, give the following definition: 'the degree of heaviness of a thing, especially as measured on a balance or weighing machine. Expressed according to units of measurement; for example, kilos, tons, etc. Apples are usually sold by weight.'

What would a child learn from such an example? Some children might be able to memorize such a definition, but would they really understand what weight meant? According to Piaget, to really understand a concept you have to be actively involved. Therefore, as in the case study 2.1, children learn about weight by holding and measuring different objects. Active involvement leads to the development of schemas or units of mental thought.

In discovery learning, the teacher or teaching assistant needs to encourage the expansion of existing schemas and the development of new schemas. Sometimes when teaching a child, it is very clear to the teacher or teaching assistant that the child has no idea or the completely wrong idea about a concept. For example, in case study 1.1 in the previous chapter, we read about Sam, a little boy who believed that squares and rectangles were the same because both shapes had four corners. At this point the teacher or teaching assistant must ask questions or create situations where the child realizes for himself that there is a contradiction between what they believe to be true, their reality, and what everyone else believes to be true, a shared reality. A discovery learning activity focusing on the differences between squares and rectangles could involve pupils, such as Sam, measuring the sides of rectangles and squares and writing these down. By participating in such an activity Sam could learn for himself the difference between squares and rectangles. It is also possible that other children can provide contrasting views. When a child experiences contrasting or differing views to his or her own, this is called socio-cognitive conflict.

In summary, discovery learning involves:

- assessing what the child knows and does not know, and
- asking questions or providing activities that create the need to expand existing schemas or to establish new schemas.

The spiral curriculum

Bruner, an American psychologist, developed the concept of the **spiral curriculum**. The spiral curriculum involves teaching the same concepts at different ages but with increasing complexity. This can be seen within the National Curriculum, where topics are introduced in the earliest years and revisited in later years but in more detail. Bruner (1963) stated that any subject can be taught effectively and in some intellectually honest form to any child at any stage of development.

Linked to the idea of the spiral curriculum are Bruner's views on how thinking develops. Bruner outlined three ways of thinking or processing information, which he called **modes of representation**. These modes develop with time. They are:

- *Enactive representation.* This form of memory can be likened to a muscle memory and begins at birth. Examples of this muscle memory would include a baby learning to grasp a rattle or a baby learning to crawl. This form of memory continues throughout adult life. Examples of this muscle memory in later life would be learning to drive.
- *Iconic mode.* This way of thinking develops from the age of one. Information is encoded or remembered in the form of mental images or pictures. Information is also remembered as smells or sounds.
- *The symbolic mode.* This way of processing information develops around the age of seven, and is a way of remembering by using symbols and codes. Examples of symbols and codes are language and mathematical rules. For example, we often learn how to do a task by remembering in words what to do; or when logging on to the internet we will remind ourselves that we need to click on a certain icon and key in a password.

According to Bruner, the way in which a subject is taught to a young child should correspond to a child's mode of representation or their current way of thinking. Bruner would say that children over seven and adults could use

Table 2.1 The spiral curriculum

Stage	Example of teaching style
Enactive. Memory is encoded in the muscles whenever the individual physically acts on its environment. This type of memory develops from birth.	A very young child could learn about weight by lifting objects. A small teddy is easier to carry around than the three-foot teddy Daddy won at the fair.
Iconic. A child between the ages of one and seven uses mental images based on sight, touch, hearing and smell.	A class of Year 1 children take turns weighing parcels of different sizes on a scale. The pupils use multi-link pieces to balance the scales.
Symbolic. Individuals of seven and above are able to represent ideas through symbols or rules.	A Year 11 class is given the following question: 'The density of air is 1.3 kg/m³. What mass of air is contained in a room measuring 2.5 m x 4 m x 10 m?'

all ways of thinking or modes of representation. Table 2.1 illustrates how the concept of weight could be taught at various ages.

Scaffolding

Vygotsky introduced the concept of scaffolding. However, in more recent years it has been psychologists such as Bruner that have developed and expanded on this idea.

As a learning support strategy, scaffolding relates to effective instruction. For Vygotsky, the language of instruction is everything. Instruction needs to correspond to the pupil's ability: when the pupil is struggling, more help is given; and when the pupil is succeeding, help is withdrawn. It is through this language of instruction that a pupil can build on their existing knowledge and understanding. The concept of scaffolding relates to Vygotsky's other key concept of the Zone of Proximal Development. The Zone of Proximal Development incorporates both what the pupils can do by themselves and what they can do with assistance. It is believed that what pupils can do today with help, in time they will be able to do by themselves. Importantly, Vygotsky stated that the most efficient type of instruction would be aimed at a developmental level just above a pupil's current level of development. To help us in an understanding of what exactly scaffolding entails, consider the dialogue in case study 2.3.

Case study 2.3

Scaffolding

Sarah (TA):	Now, Jessica, choose a parcel.

Jessica picks up the heaviest parcel.

Sarah (TA):	Now tell me, Jessica, is the parcel very heavy or very light?
Jessica (pupil):	It is very light.

Sarah gives Jessica the lightest parcel.

Sarah (TA):	Hold this parcel now. Which is the heavier parcel?
Jessica:	They are both light – no, they are both heavy.
Sarah (TA):	Now which is it, heavy or light?
Jessica:	Um . . . I don't know.
Sarah (TA):	What do we mean by heavy? What is heavy?
Jessica:	Um . . .

Sarah (TA):	Have you ever seen an elephant?
Jessica:	Oh yes, I love going to the zoo. Granny took me there last Easter.
Sarah (TA):	Could you pick up an elephant?
Jessica (laughs):	Oh no, elephants are too big!
Sarah (TA):	So an elephant would be too heavy for you to pick up. Could you pick up a feather?
Jessica:	Of course! Feathers are easy to pick up. I love feathers. Granny has feathers in her hat.
Sarah (TA):	So a feather is easy to pick up and, well, you couldn't pick up an elephant. So we could say a feather is light and an elephant is heavy. Now, what did I say an elephant is?

(Waits for Jessica to fill in the rest of the information.)

Jessica:	An elephant is heavy and a feather is light.
Sarah (TA):	Good! That is right. You are really thinking about this. Now hold these two parcels. Which is heavier and which is lighter?
Jessica:	Um ...
Sarah (TA):	Which is easier to pick up and which is harder to pick up?
Jessica:	This is easier to pick up and this one is harder to pick up.
Sarah (TA):	If that parcel is the easier to pick up, we could say that the parcel is ... ?
Jessica:	Light.
Sarah (TA):	Good girl! So now, which is the heavy parcel?
Jessica:	This one, because it is the hardest to pick up.

What this dialogue illustrates is that Jessica needed help to understand the concepts of heavy and light and that this help took the form of carefully selected questions and comments. This example illustrates effective instruction. Effective instruction is not just telling the pupil what is the right and wrong answer, but through language helping them to come to an understanding of the concepts for themselves. This example also shows that when a pupil is struggling, more help is given; and when they are succeeding, less help is given. You could also say that this example illustrates Piaget's idea of assimilation because the teaching assistant is trying to have Jessica relate the concepts of heavy and light to what she already knows about elephants and feathers. The difference between Piaget and Vygotsky is that Vygotsky places more emphasis on the language of communication.

Dynamic assessment: observing pupil's responses

Dynamic assessment involves an adult interacting with a pupil in order to help them develop their thinking and learning skills. This approach involves an adult working one-on-one with a pupil on a task or problem and carefully noting both what they say to support the pupil's learning and the pupil's responses. Dynamic assessment provides useful information on how the adult supports or modifies the task, and what the adult learns about the pupil's potential to succeed. According to Fuchs *et al.* (2007), dynamic assessment involves:

1. Setting a problem.
2. Observing the pupil's response to the set problem, specifically noting the pupil's reaction and the learning skills that are already present and well established.
3. Giving the pupil support when the pupil experiences difficulties. It is important to note specifically what support is given and how the pupil responds to the support.
4. Giving the pupil a similar problem, i.e. a problem at the same level. The adult then observes whether new skills practised in the first problem have been learnt and applied to the new problem.

This technique is often used by educational psychologists but the emphasis on carefully noting what you say and exactly how the pupil responds is an essential component of delivering feedback to the teacher. (For further information on dynamic assessment, see pages 104–5, and for further information on feedback, see pages 71, 96–7 and 163.)

Thinking deeply

Think of a pupil you support on a regular basis and think of your feedback to the teacher. What specific factors do you feed back to the teacher?

Do you comment on:

Whether the pupil had met the learning objectives?

How the pupil approached the task? For example, were they lively, alert, confident, impulsive or easily distracted?

How willing the pupil was to accept support?

Whether the pupil relied on any particular learning style? For example, visual, auditory or kinaesthetic?

What strategies the pupil used?

Whether the pupil was aware of the strategies they used?

What motivated the pupil?

Whether the pupil could apply the skills learnt in one situation to another similar situation?

If you were the teaching assistant in case study 2.3, what feedback would you give to the teacher?

Behavioural analysis, task analysis and shaping

As we have mentioned before, behaviourists believe that behaviour is controlled by reinforcement (rewards) and punishment. Certainly within school settings we can think of many examples of such, from the giving out of stickers or merit points to the good old detention.

Feedback and constructive feedback

Feedback from a teacher or teaching assistant, depending on the nature of the feedback, could be considered either a reward or a punishment. Praise is a common type of feedback used by teachers and teaching assistants. However, for praise to be effective it must be seen as genuine by the pupils. For example, telling the pupil that their work is good when *they* know and *you* know that it isn't, is not very helpful. Perhaps it would be better to focus on one aspect of their work that is good and to praise that. This point leads on to another aspect of giving praise: the need to make it clear to the pupil what the praise is for. If a pupil knows what they are being praised for and they find the praise rewarding, then they are more likely to repeat that behaviour.

What is often the most difficult aspect of giving feedback is what to say about a pupil's work when it is clear that they have got completely the wrong idea. **Constructive feedback** is the art of acknowledging what a pupil has done in a manner that is seen as helpful by the pupil. Often constructive feedback involves stating something that the pupil has done well and then focusing on what they need to do next. For example, in case study 2.2 where the pupils were having difficulties coming to grips with essay writing, the teaching assistant could say: 'It is obvious you have spent a lot of effort and time thinking about essay writing, but maybe it would be helpful to try it this way.' Such a statement would be an example of constructive feedback. Constructive feedback would *not* be saying to this group of pupils: 'How many times does the teacher have to explain essay-writing skills before it sinks in?' Obviously such a statement would only serve to undermine the pupils' confidence in their own learning.

Analysing behaviour

As we have said before, the reason behind giving out rewards and punishments is that rewards should increase a desired behaviour and punishment should decrease an undesired behaviour. But behaviour can be complex, because what is a reward or a punishment depends on the individual. According to this theory, if a pupil behaves in a certain way it is because the behaviour gives the pupil some sort of pay-off. This is true for inappropriate or even very disturbed behaviour. In order to determine why a pupil behaves in a certain way, it is necessary to stand back and observe. In observing behaviour it is important to:

* note what happens before the behaviour; this is sometimes called the antecedent
* describe the behaviour, and
* describe the consequences of the behaviour.

Let us re-examine case study 1.2 (mentioned in Chapter 1), but this time with a few more details.

If we look at the consequences of James's behaviour, we see that James received a lot of attention from his peers and escaped from the mock test. We could guess that James finds both these consequences rewarding. It would also be beneficial to ask James what he considers to be a reward.

How to change behaviour: shaping and task analysis

Once it has been determined what reinforcement or reward is responsible for a pupil's behaviour, then the teacher needs to consider how to reward appropriate behaviour and how to ignore inappropriate behaviour, keeping in mind what the pupil finds rewarding. According to this theory, to change behaviour you need to shape or reward desired behaviour. However, before you begin to shape new behaviour it is helpful to do what is called a **task analysis**. A task analysis involves looking at a skill which you would like the pupil to have and breaking that skill into steps or component parts. For example, what skills does a pupil need to have to be able to weigh two objects and decide whether one is heavier than the other? To do this task a pupil would need to:

* understand the concepts of heavy and light
* be familiar with scales and how to use scales
* know how to read the scales and tell how much an object weighs.

Table 2.2 An example of analysing behaviour

Time	Antecedent (what happens before the behaviour)	Behaviour	Consequence
10:05	Teacher tells class that they are going to do a mock GCSE test.		
10:07		James reaches into his pocket and pulls out a beetle, which he puts on his desk.	
10:08			Teacher observes the beetle and says, 'James, remove that beetle from this class at once!'
10:08		James falls on his knees and pleads with the teacher: 'No, sir, this is my best friend, Freddy. I can't go on without Freddy!'	Class are in stitches laughing at what has happened.
10:09			The teacher yells: 'Right, James, I have told you before – I will not tolerate you acting up in class. Stand outside right now!'
10:10		James picks up his beetle, smirks and leaves the classroom.	

Can you think of any more? Perhaps you could break the above steps into even smaller steps.

Let's take another example. What skills does a pupil need to have in order to be able to successfully sit a mock maths test? Certainly they would need to:

- be able to read and understand questions or have these questions read to them
- have relevant information relating to maths stored in their memory (this step could be further broken down into relevant information on specific aspects of maths, e.g. fractions and percentages)
- be able to remember the information when required.

Can you think of any more steps?

If a pupil cannot do a task, it is important first to determine what parts of the task they can do and what parts of the task they are having difficulty with. Let us return to the example of James and his beetle. Let us imagine that the reason for James's disruptive behaviour is because he knows he cannot do the work, but doesn't want others to know that he cannot do it. First, it is important to assess what James *can* do, i.e. to carry out a task analysis. Once it has been determined what James can do and also what James finds difficult, then achievable goals can be set. If James was given realistic goals to work on in class and if he was given praise for achieving these goals, then perhaps he might begin to feel better about being in maths – and then maybe he need not act up to escape maths. Over time, the expectations of what James can do in maths could be increased slowly at a rate suitable for him, so that in time he could confidently sit a mock GCSE exam.

Shaping of a behaviour involves starting with a pupil's existing capabilities and gradually asking more and more of them until they can eventually perform a required task or skill. It is essential that for shaping to work, what is asked of the pupil at each stage is achievable and that they are rewarded for their achievements. The pupil must be competent and confident at a previous stage before they can proceed to the next. Shaping is a technique that can be applied to such diverse tasks as tying shoelaces, making toast, doing multiplication, sitting still for twenty minutes and writing an essay.

Multi-sensory approaches

Multi-sensory approaches involve teaching a subject in such a way that all senses are being used (see Table 2.3). This learning strategy is often used when teaching pupils with dyslexia. Multi-sensory approaches are based on the fact that while some people can learn by a variety of means equally well, others have a preferred learning style. In case study 2.1, the concepts of weighing and heavy and light were taught by using the following approaches:

• Touch and movement were used when pupils had an opportunity to hold parcels to see what was light and what was heavy. Touch and movement were also used when pupils had to put the parcels on scales and balance them with multi-link pieces.
• Visual senses were used as the pupils were watching as the parcels were weighed.
• Auditory senses were used as pupils were listening to what the teaching assistant and other pupils had to say.

Specific skills

Questioning

Teachers and teaching assistants will often use questions as a learning support strategy. Questions are asked for a number of reasons, including to:

• check understanding or find out what pupils already know
• review and revise previously taught material by recalling what they have learned
• encourage thinking, and to encourage pupils to ask questions themselves
• gain pupils' attention and make sure that pupils are listening
• draw in shyer pupils
• find out why pupils aren't working as they should, and
• teach a topic through pupils' answers to questions (Brown and Wragg 1993).

Work on questioning has revealed that there are different types of questions. One dimension of questioning is referred to as **open** versus **closed** or **narrow** versus **broad**. These dimensions describe the types of answers that are required from the pupil. For example, a closed or narrow question

Table 2.3 The senses and their use

Type of learner	Senses used	Examples of preferred learning activities
Kinaesthetic	Touch, movement	Doing things, making models, tracing letters in sand
Visual	Sight	Reading, watching videos
Auditory	Hearing	Listening to tapes, listening to teacher talking

would be, 'Who is the Prime Minister of the United Kingdom?' To that question there is only one answer. On the other hand, an open or broad question would be: 'What would you like to do on your summer holidays?' Obviously here there is no one right answer and the answers given could be quite elaborate. Another dimension of questioning is referred to as **recall** versus **thought**. Recall questions check on existing knowledge and observation, while thought questions stimulate the development of new ideas and in that respect create new knowledge. It is also important to consider whether the questions are clear and easily understood, i.e. do the pupils understand what they are being asked? The manner, or tone of voice, in which the questions are asked is also important. Are the questions seen as an opportunity to participate in a stimulating classroom discussion or are they a means of catching out those pupils who are not paying attention? There is an art to questioning – a good questioner will match the style of their questions to the demands of the lesson and the characteristics of the learner. As we have seen, the use of carefully constructed or well thought-out questions are an important part of scaffolding. To recap what we have so far learned regarding questions, let us look at Table 2.4.

Table 2.4 Types of question

Type	Examples	Advantage	Disadvantage
Recall narrow	Who is the Prime Minister? Are cats' tails long or short?	Assesses knowledge or observation.	Need to match questions to pupils. If the questions are too simple, the pupils might appear puzzled as they might think it is a trick, or they might become bored and act up.
Recall broad	What did you do in the summer holidays?		
Narrow thought	Do you think the story has a happy ending? Are spiders useful?	Possibility of creating new knowledge.	Need to be carefully constructed.
Broad thought	How do you think the story will end? What would be the impact on the ecosystem if spiders became extinct?		

Brown and Wragg (1993) identified a number of common errors in questioning including:

- asking too many questions
- asking a question only to answer it yourself
- not giving pupils enough time to think about the answer to a question (it is important to allow for sufficient 'wait time')
- always asking the same pupils
- asking too easy or too difficult questions
- not responding to wrong answers
- ignoring answers, and
- failing to build on or link pupils' answers to questions.

Brown and Wragg (1993) also outlined a manner of including questions in learning sessions. These are detailed next.

Structuring

Structuring involves introducing or explaining the topic of the lesson or support session by asking pupils questions and expanding on their answers. Structuring questions can be used with a class of pupils, a small group or individually. In a sense, structuring is used to set the scene and tell the pupils what they are going to be doing.

Pitching and putting

This involves deciding what types of question you are going to ask and when you are going to ask them. Here there is a need to match your questions to the content of the lesson and the characteristics or abilities of your pupils. For example, a question such as: 'What would be the implication on the ecosystem if spiders became extinct?' would be appropriate for Year 10 pupils, but not reception children. Perhaps a better question for reception pupils would be: 'Are spiders useful?'

Distributing and directing

This involves deciding to whom you are going to address your questions. Distributing means that you are not only asking the most confident or the brightest pupils in the class. In this way, questioning can encourage greater participation; however, care needs to be taken with very shy or withdrawn pupils.

As a teaching assistant, you have a role to play in encouraging responses, as case study 2.4 illustrates.

Case study 2.4

Encouraging responses

The Year 7 pupil I was supporting has no confidence in himself or his abilities and always seems to fear getting something wrong, although I often remind him that it's OK to be wrong. At the end of the lesson, the teacher was going through the answers as a class. All the other pupils were putting their hands up to answer. When I approached my pupil quietly and discreetly and encouraged him to answer the questions, his reply was: 'But what if I am wrong?' I said that he could also be right. Then I reminded him again that it doesn't matter if his answer wasn't correct, and pointed out to him that not all the other pupils were giving right answers all the time. I then walked away and on the next question the teacher asked, my pupil reluctantly put his hand halfway up and when asked, he got it right. It was so rewarding to see his face light up. After that there was no stopping him, although he would look over for a little nod of approval from myself.

Pauses and paces

There is an advantage to pausing after a question as this allows pupils time to think and encourages greater participation. This also avoids the pitfall of overwhelming the pupils with too many questions.

Prompting or probing

Prompts or **probes** are defined as follow-up questions you give pupils when the answer you get from them is not quite what you are looking for.

Prompts can be made in the following manner:

- Rephrasing the question in simpler language. For example, in a literacy session you might initially ask: 'How have the characters developed through this chapter?' If the pupils look at you with blank expressions then you might rephrase the question as: 'How have the characters changed? What were they like at the beginning of the chapter? What were they like at the end?'
- Breaking the initial question into smaller and simpler questions, and eventually leading back to the initial question. For example, during a

discussion on the usefulness of spiders in a reception class you might break the question: 'Are spiders useful?' into 'Who has seen a spider?' 'What do spiders do?' and then 'Do you think spiders are useful?'

- Reviewing or reminding pupils of the information they need to answer the question. For example, if you are supporting a pupil writing an essay on the characteristics of rainforests and the pupil seems not to know where to begin, you might break the essay into a series of questions that they can answer. One question might be: 'How is a tropical rainforest different from the New Forest, the place where you went on holiday last year?'

Probes are slightly different in that they are additional questions given to try to get the pupil to give you the more specific information you are looking for. For example, if a pupil replied that spiders are really useful, you might say: 'Well, can you think of an example of how they are useful?'

Questioning the impact of questions

Think about the theory you have read so far and relate this to your own experiences to complete the table below:

Question	Is the question open or closed?	Does the question check existing knowledge (recall) or stimulate thought?	Provide an example of when you used this type of question.
Does anyone have a question?			
Can you give an example . . .			
How do we know that . . .			
What would be another point of view?			
Can you tell me more?			
How did you arrive at that answer?			

(continued)

(continued)

Question	Is the question open or closed?	Does the question check existing knowledge (recall) or stimulate thought?	Provide an example of when you used this type of question.
Why do you think that?			
What do you mean by . . .			
What if someone was to suggest . . .			

Thinking deeply

Choose one session in which you are supporting a pupil or group of pupils and afterwards try to remember and write down the various questions you asked. Alternatively, you could use a digital recorder or camcorder to record what you actually said. After the session, review your questions.

What type of questions did you ask?

How effective were the questions you asked?

Listening and responding

Here you need to listen to the pupils and expand on the pupils' explanations or ask other pupils to expand. In this way you are teaching a subject through the questions you give and the answers you receive back. In responding to a pupil's answer, you could incorporate another pupil's previous answer. This is a way of valuing their contributions as well as reviewing what has been previously said. For example, in a discussion on spiders with a small group of pupils you might say: 'Now John has said that spiders catch flies in their webs and Andy said that he once saw a giant fly caught in a web, so we can agree with Amy that spiders are useful in catching insects.'

Explaining

One stage that could benefit from further comments is how to introduce or explain a topic. Wragg and Brown (1993) suggest to:

- Identify key concepts. For example, in starting a learning activity the teacher or teaching assistant might outline to the group or class what they are going to discuss: 'Today we are going to talk about bears and where they live.' Asking the pupils what they already know or by reviewing what has been said in previous lessons provides a framework for pupils to understand new material by connecting it to information they already know.
- Present ideas clearly and in a logical order.
- Use language and tone of voice appropriate for the pupil audience.
- Use a range of strategies to explain key concepts. This could include books, pictures and activities.

Figure 8 The benefits of observational learning.

Modelling

In his social learning theory, Bandura talked about observational learning involving how pupils watch and learn. Teaching assistants can use this strategy on several levels. For example, at the simplest level, a teaching assistant could shadow other teaching assistants and see what they do and how they relate to pupils. This is always very useful for the teaching assistant who has just started.

On another level, teaching assistants can use the 'watch and learn' approach to show pupils what they should be doing. They can demonstrate the activity themselves or point out other pupils who are very good at that skill. For example, they might say, 'See how Amy is holding that pencil' or 'Just look at how John turns on his computer' or 'Watch how I am going to add these sums on the whiteboard.'

To encourage good behaviour, a teaching assistant could point out the good behaviour of another pupil; this pupil would be serving as a positive role model. Remember what Bandura said about role models: they are more effective if the pupil can relate to them, if they are admired and respected by others, and if the pupil has seen the role model being rewarded for good behaviour. Take case study 2.5, for example:

Case study 2.5

Rewarding good behaviour

The teacher asked me to hand out the worksheets. One by one I gave out the worksheets. After the tenth child took their sheet, one little boy actually said in a loud voice: 'Thank you, Miss.' I immediately replied, 'Well done, Bill! Excellent manners!' and I then gave him a sticker. This caused some sort of impact on the others as they all then thanked me for their work. Of course, I then had to give all of the pupils who said thank you a sticker.

A further distinction has been made between mastery models and coping models. **Mastery models** are pupils who can easily do the task. Sometimes it is helpful to ask a pupil who is struggling to watch another pupil who is an expert to see how they do it and pick up tips. However, if there is too much of a difference between what the pupils can do, then the pupil who is struggling may feel that the task is just too difficult and that they will never be able to do it. In these situations it is more helpful to ask a pupil to watch a **coping model** who themselves has difficulties with learning and makes mistakes, but who doesn't give up when they experience difficulties. Coping models are pupils who learn from their mistakes and move forward.

On a final note, teaching assistants can act as effective role models for the behaviour which they expect and wish to see in the pupils they support.

Emotional responses

In the previous chapter we talked about conditioned emotional responses and how for learning to be effective it must not be associated with negative emotions such as fear and anxiety. A teaching assistant can help the pupil to feel at ease and comfortable in the learning situation. When a pupil feels emotionally safe, they can take a chance on trying to tackle those subjects they find difficult. If pupils feel emotionally safe they can risk failure. A key factor in enabling a pupil to feel emotionally secure and safe is to develop a relationship with the pupil. But relationships take time, as case study 2.6 illustrates.

Case study 2.6

Building up trust takes time

Chelsea is incredibly shy and lacks confidence. I knew that to get anywhere with her I first had to gain her trust. I sat next to Chelsea. However, I first asked her if it was OK for me to sit there. She nodded that it was. My first objective was to make her relaxed and happy. I did and said things which I hoped would make her smile. At first I did all the talking; I explained what she needed to do and if Chelsea needed to answer me she would nod or shake her head. Gradually as Chelsea got to know me better she started answering yes or no and finally she started talking normally.

One advantage of having a relationship with someone is that it becomes easier to say those hard things, as one teaching assistant explains:

Case study 2.7

Being able to be honest

I constantly tell my pupils how I think their work is progressing. I like to use praise and always do so when appropriate. If, however, they have not worked to their full potential or maybe their behaviour was not appropriate I let them know I am disappointed, that I know they can do better. We talk about why there is a problem and try to solve it together.

Specific strategies

One of the areas mentioned in Chapter 1 was a pupil's awareness of their own memory processes and the strategies that they use to help them learn a task. (For further information on metamemory, see pages 56–7.) While more able pupils just seem to pick these strategies up, pupils who are struggling could benefit from specific help in such strategies. **Process-based instruction** is a strategy that specifically attempts to teach pupils how to solve problems systematically (Ashman and Conway 1993) by teaching pupils how to plan their work. Pupils are taught to ask themselves a series of ordered questions:

- Where should I start?
- How do I start?
- What is the essential sequence of actions needed? or What steps are involved in completing this assignment?
- Is my plan working as I expected?
- Have I completed the task correctly?
- Have I finished or do I need to go back and do some additional work?

Case study 2.8

Process-based instruction

In case study 2.2, Donna was working with a small group in a Year 9 English class. The pupils' task was to write an essay comparing the differences between two advertisements in terms of form, purpose, audience, content, language and presentation. Let us imagine that we are listening into Donna's session.

Donna (TA):	When we do an assignment, we are going to ask ourselves a series of questions.

(She shows the group a list of questions, which she has prepared earlier. Each member of the group has a list of these questions. Donna is following the process-based instruction approach.)

Donna (TA):	What is the first question?
Sharon:	It says 'Where should I start?' Well, I don't know.
Brad:	My mum always tells me to read the questions first.
Donna (TA):	That's a good idea. It is always a good idea to start off by asking yourself what you are supposed to do.
Sharon:	Write an essay about comparing two advertisements on the language of persuasion.

Donna (TA):	Yes, that's right. So now let's see what is the next question. 'How do I start?'
Sharon:	Well, Miss, that is the hard bit. I don't know what the question even means.
Donna (TA):	Brad, Kim, John, do you have any ideas?
John:	I haven't a clue and (under his breath) I couldn't care less.
Brad:	All I know is that I would rather be in Tenerife.
John:	Yeah, I'm for that.
Donna (TA):	OK, so would I.

(Everyone laughs.)

Donna (TA):	But imagine that if you didn't know anything about Tenerife – how would you know whether you wanted to go there or not?
Kim:	I think I get it. It's like deciding where to go at the weekend. If Amy says it's a good place then you know it is, but if my mum thinks I would enjoy it, well, then I would never go there.
Donna (TA):	Yes, that relates to this. In this case, the only way we can check out whether the hotel in Tenerife is what we want is by what the advert says.
Sharon:	So, Miss, we are supposed to look at the ads and say whether they would convince us whether to go or not? I think I understand now what we are supposed to do. What next, Miss?
Donna (TA):	What's the next question?
Brad:	'What steps are involved in the assignment?'
Donna (TA):	Well, I would make a plan. In an essay we first need an introduction. An introduction explains what we are going to do, then we need a middle bit, discussing the facts, and then we need the end, where we state our feelings and conclusions.
Sharon:	So for the introduction we say we are going to talk about the adverts.
Brad:	It's more than that; we are going to compare the adverts.
Kim:	So all we have do is just write down what we are going to do.
Donna (TA):	Yes. Let's all get out a piece of paper and write that down.
John:	What down?

Kim:	In this essay we are going to compare adverts on Tenerife.
Donna (TA):	Now that we have got that down what are we going to do next?
Sharon:	Miss, we need the middle bit – the facts.
Brad:	Well, this ad talks about a place my parents would go to. I wouldn't be caught dead at a place like that.
Donna (TA):	Why did you say that?
Brad:	Just look at what they say about formal dress for dinner.
Donna (TA):	Well, Brad, that is the type of detail you would need in the middle. And then after writing all the facts down, you need to write a conclusion about what you think of the ads.
Teacher:	Class, you have got two minutes to finish what you are doing.
Donna (TA):	Now I think we have made a good start. If you get stuck with your essay, look at the list of questions and we will talk about it next time.

Thinking deeply

How has Donna made use of strategies relating to metamemory and process-based instruction? (Hint: refer to pages 56–7 and 84.)

Is there anything that Donna could have done to improve the session?

What details should Donna feed back to the teacher? (Hint: refer to page 70.)

Reflection

In this chapter we have covered many strategies and specific skills used to promote effective learning. Teaching would be much easier if there was one 'right' strategy, but hopefully by now you have realized that no one strategy is 'better' than another – the 'best' strategy to use will depend very much on the situation at the time and the individual pupil with whom you are working. In a sense, discovering what works and doesn't work is a matter of trial and error and that is where reflection can be very useful.

Case study 2.9

Reflecting on a primary school lesson

Jane works with a small group of five Year 4 pupils on ALS (Additional Literacy Support). Jane completed the following workplace log.

> I was in the library working with five children on ALS. I first reminded them of the rules of paying attention and that if we want to talk we put our hands up. I told the children we were going to play a game which involved picking a question out of a bag and asking the person next to them that question but we had to answer the question in a complete sentence.

Me:	How old are you?
Rory:	Eight.
Me:	Is that a sentence or a phrase?
Rory:	Phrase.
Me:	Good. A phrase is just one word that doesn't make complete sense. A sentence begins with a capital letter, ends with a full stop and makes complete sense.
Rory:	How many legs does a dog have?
Omar:	My dog has three legs.
Me:	Does it really? OK – you ask the next question.
Omar:	What is your favourite type of ice-cream?
Kyle:	My favourite type of ice-cream is chocolate.

The game continued and it went very well, that is except for Grace. Grace had real problems with this task. It started when Rory asked Grace a question.

Rory:	How many days are there in the week?
Grace:	Seven.
Rory:	No, that's a phrase. You got it wrong and that was an easy question!

I could see that Grace was looking upset.

Me:	Well, Rory, was that a kind remark to make to Grace? OK, Rory, you ask me a question.

Rory pulled a question out of the bag and asked me, 'What is your favourite meal?' I said, 'Fish and chips.' I deliberately said the wrong answer. The children all laughed, including Grace, and I said, 'See, Rory, this is difficult.' Well, at that point we had to go back to the class.

> On reflection I think the session went just fine, although Grace had problems with the task. In fact she never got one question right. I think I made her feel better by making a mistake myself but that didn't help her with the task.

Thinking deeply

What other questions, prompts or probes could Jane ask to extend the pupil's understanding of the difference between a phrase and a sentence?

How do you think Grace felt about always getting the questions wrong?

How could you develop Grace's understanding? (Hint: you could refer to Piaget, or task analysis, or scaffolding, or dynamic assessment or the use of questioning as a way forward.)

Chapter 3

Learning styles

Barriers to effective learning

In previous chapters we have discussed potential barriers to learning and ways of overcoming them. Piaget would talk about maturational readiness, i.e. a child at a certain age will become able to understand and perform certain academic tasks. So, for example, a teacher might explain to the mother of a Year 1 pupil that the reason her child was having difficulty with reading was that perhaps the child was just not ready, but when they were ready it would just fall into place. Vygotsky, on the other hand, would talk about the importance of matching the language of communication to the child's abilities and level of understanding. For Vygotsky, teaching is the art of effective communication. If the explanation is not understandable to the pupil then learning cannot occur. Other barriers to learning that have already been mentioned are the ineffective use of questions, the association of particular classes or subjects with negative emotions such as fear and anxiety, and the reinforcement of disruptive and inappropriate behaviour. However, another important characteristic of the pupil that would affect their ability to learn revolves around what has been described as **learning styles**.

Learning styles

If you were asked to describe your ideal lesson, what would it be? Would you opt for a stimulating lecture, an audio–visual presentation or a hands-on workshop? Similarly, when you study at home, do you like absolute peace and quiet, some easy-listening background music, or do you prefer to work with the television and radio blaring? What we are talking about here are learning styles. A learning style can be defined as the different and preferred ways in which children and adults think and learn. Although all pupils have their own preferred learning style, the question is to what extent is the delivery of the teaching material matched to each pupil's unique learning style. Often pupils do not have a choice in how teaching material is presented; therefore it is just as well that most pupils, though having preferences in learning styles, can put up with and learn in a variety of situations.

However, some pupils with special educational needs seem to learn best when information is presented in a certain way. This is where knowledge of learning styles can lead to effective learning support strategies.

Types of learning style

Dunn and Dunn (1993a and b) based the following review of different types of learning style on extensive research.

Processing information styles

- *Global versus analytic.* This refers to how a pupil prefers to approach a topic. A global approach would see the pupil preferring to first have an overview of the topic. Globals need to see the big picture before they can concentrate on the details. On the other hand, analytics find the whole picture too overwhelming and prefer to approach a topic by starting at the beginning and proceeding step by step in an ordered manner to the conclusion.
- *Impulsive versus reflective.* This refers to the amount of time a pupil takes to think about a task before they start to work. Some pupils prefer to take their time and seriously consider the task before they begin. The difficulty with this approach is that while the pupil thinks about the task nothing is actually written down. This can be discouraging both to the pupil and to the teacher. At the other extreme, some pupils don't even take time to read the instructions properly; they just jump in. Obviously pupils at both extremes will have difficulty successfully completing the task. Perhaps teachers or teaching assistants need to encourage a certain amount of thinking and planning time before the pupil starts to write.

Environmental learning styles

- *Preferred level of sound or background noise.* Individuals differ in regard to what level of noise they find most helpful when learning or studying.

- *Preferred room temperature.* Some individuals prefer a cool room, while others prefer a warm or hot environment.
- *Preferred classroom design.* Different learners prefer different seating arrangements. Do you prefer to study sitting in a traditional desk and chair, or do you prefer a more informal environment of chairs and tables being arranged in groups or a semicircle? Do you prefer learning while sitting on a couch, or on the floor?
- *Preferred level of lighting.* Some learners prefer to work in soft or dim light, while others prefer a brightly lit space.

To some extent the teacher can control factors such as noise levels, room temperature, lighting and classroom design. These factors have an important role to play in supporting learning for pupils with ASC, ADHD and dyslexia. (For further information on these additional learning needs, see Chapter 4.)

Emotional learning styles

- *Preferred degree of responsibility.* Does the pupil prefer to work independently *without any* adult supervision, feedback or guidance? Does the pupil prefer to have *some* adult supervision, feedback and guidance? Does the pupil prefer *frequent* adult supervision, feedback and guidance? This is an area that has particular relevance to teaching assistants. Of course, the key here is knowing the pupils you work with.

Case study 3.1

Recognizing emotional learning styles

Sarah (a Year 9 pupil) always wants me to sit right beside her, whereas John (Year 9, in a different class) hates me sitting beside him. It took me a while to figure John out. When I sat next to him he wouldn't even look at me and he just mumbled 'Yes' or 'No' to my questions. Now I sit at the back and John and I have this system. When he looks at me, I know he wants me to come and help him, but I only go to his desk if I see him looking at me. It's all about 'street cred'. We get on great now, because John knows that I am there if he needs me.

- *Preferred degree of structure.* Does the pupil want to be told in precise detail what the learning task is and exactly how they should do it, or does the pupil prefer to be given choices in both what to do and how to do it? Again it seems that knowing the preferences of the pupil whom you are supporting is important.

- *Degree of persistence individuals bring to educational task.* The level of persistence a pupil brings to a task depends on the pupil's attention span, ability and interest. Some pupils will prefer to work on one task at a time, preferring to finish one task before they move on to the next, while some pupils like to have many tasks on the go at the same time.
- *Degree of motivation individuals bring to educational task.* This refers to how interested a pupil is in learning at school. Some pupils will be self-motivated; they have a deep internal need to learn. Motivation to learn in this case is said to be **intrinsic**. However, other pupils are motivated to learn only if the subject interests them. Some pupils' motivation to go to school is that they can be near their friends. For these pupils, feedback and praise from their friends are an important source of motivation. Knowing what motivates a pupil to learn can have practical applications.

Case study 3.2

Finding what motivates

Sam (a Year 1 pupil) just did not like to read, or at least he didn't seem to like to read from the books we were using in class. Then his mum mentioned to the teacher that he was particularly interested in stars and black holes. Well, the teacher and I searched the library for all the books we could find on these topics. Sam still has to read the books from the reading scheme but now, as a reward for finishing his class book, the next book we read is one of his choosing.

In this example, Sam's motivation to learn about stars and black holes was used to develop his reading.

Preferences in social patterns

This learning style refers to whether a pupil prefers to:

- work alone
- work as a member of a pair or a small or large group
- work with adult supervision
- have variety in regard to whom they work with, *or* take comfort in set routines and work patterns.

Of course all these preferences may vary from class to class or from subject to subject.

Perceptual learning styles

Perceptual learning style refers to how pupils take in and process information. Specifically, we are looking at what senses (e.g. sight, sound, touch) are being used to process information. Understanding the different perceptual learning styles is important because pupils prefer to be taught and learn more when the teaching activities match their **perceptual style**.

- **Visual learners** prefer teaching activities which involve seeing and watching. This type of pupil will learn by watching demonstrations and videos, or by looking at pictures, maps and diagrams.
- **Auditory learners** prefer teaching activities that involve hearing and listening. Such pupils will learn best by listening to tapes, lectures or music.
- **Kinaesthetic learners** learn through physical movement and touching. Such pupils would prefer hands-on activities.

Though most individuals will have one main perceptual style, it is possible to have different perceptual styles depending on the task involved. The following questions, according to Rose (1987), can help identify your perceptual style.

Identify your own perceptual learning style
When you spell:

a   Do you try to visualize or see the word in your mind?
b   Do you sound out the word, i.e. break the word into individual sound units?
c   Do you need to write the word down to see if it feels right?

When you read:

a   Do you see images in your mind?
b   Do you enjoy reading plays? Do you hear the characters talking in your head?
c   Are the only books you read action stories or 'how to' books? Would you rather do things than read?

When you are putting something together:

a   Do you need to look at the directions and diagrams?
b   Do you need to have someone tell you what to do, step by step?
c   Do you skip the directions and just figure it out as you go along?

Scoring
   If you answered mainly a, then you are a visual learner.
   If you answered mainly b, then you are an auditory learner.
   If you answered mainly c, then you are a kinaesthetic/tactile learner.

Other preferences that can affect learning

- *Time of day.* Most people will feel they work better at certain times. Some people will say they are morning people, while others feel they are at their best very late in the evening. However, most of the decisions in regard to what subject is taught when will be made by the teacher or on a school level.
- *Food and drink intake.* Many people will say that they feel they can concentrate better when they have had a cup of coffee and some individuals feel they study better when they are eating or chewing something. However, most schools will have strict rules of conduct regarding these issues.
- *Need for mobility or moving around.* This refers to an individual's preference for moving their body while being involved in a learning task. Sometimes a pupil is not aware of the degree to which they are moving or fidgeting. These individuals might say that fidgeting actually helps them to concentrate. However, another pupil might say that having someone fidgeting next to them puts them off studying. Some pupils prefer to sit still while learning and studying. Again schools will have rules concerning pupils' obligation to remain in their seats.

Adapting learning support strategies to accommodate different types of learning style

An individual's learning style is of interest to teachers and teaching assistants for a number of reasons. In particular, if a pupil is not learning, it could be that the way information is presented does not match their preferred learning style.

As a teacher or teaching assistant you might look at this information and say, 'Great! All we need to do is figure out a pupil's learning style and then teach them accordingly.' This sounds a good idea. But like many good ideas, applying this knowledge to the classroom is not without its difficulties. Already in this chapter you have read that there are many types of learning styles. If we tried to describe an individual pupil's learning style, taking in as many types as possible, it could be quite complex. For example, we might find that Jason:

- has a visual learning style for spelling
- is somewhat impulsive, i.e. he tends to start tasks without fully understanding what he has to do
- is an analytical learner, i.e. he likes to learn step by step
- prefers a hot, brightly lit classroom
- prefers frequent adult supervision, and
- has a need to move or fidget constantly.

Of course this becomes even more complex because, to be fair, we should be measuring the learning style of every pupil in a class. And if every pupil has their own unique preferred way of learning, how is it be possible to meet everyone's needs at the same time? At best, all most teachers and teaching assistants can do is to teach using a variety of approaches, therefore pleasing some of the pupils at least some of the time.

The question also arises as to whether some learning styles are better than others. Certainly as children progress through the school system, teaching seems to favour learners who can sit quietly in their seats and take in information presented in a traditional auditory format. So you could say that it is good for pupils to have to learn in many ways because having multiple learning skills would prepare them for life where they cannot always choose the manner in which they have to learn.

When working with pupils who have designated learning difficulties, it is important to recognize that all pupils will have an individual profile of strengths and weaknesses. Often teachers will first attempt to teach to strengths, i.e. to use a pupil's preferred style of learning. In Chapter 4 we will look at how pupils with Down's syndrome were best taught to read by using a visual approach, i.e. learning to read by using the 'Look and Say' method. However, it is also important that a pupil be taught a variety of strategies and ways of learning.

Nevertheless, it is still helpful to find out your pupils' learning styles. But how are learning styles measured? Traditionally, learning styles have been measured by asking pupils questions about how they like to learn. The problem with this approach is that some pupils with special educational needs might not have the ability to answer the questions or the awareness of how they learn best. In this case, the best way forward is for a teacher or teaching assistant to observe the pupil's behaviour in a variety of learning situations – for example, working in groups versus working alone, having frequent adult help versus being left alone to get on with it, or preferring to have visual, auditory, kinaesthetic activities – and make notes about which conditions result in the most effective learning.

Thinking deeply

Nova reported that at her school a learning style quiz was filled out by all the pupils at the beginning of the year. All the pupils seemed to enjoy finding out whether they were visual or auditory or kinaesthetic learners. It was hoped that knowing their individual learning style would contribute to the pupils becoming more independent autonomous learners. However, what happened was that now when certain tasks were introduced, pupils would respond by saying: 'I can't do that worksheet – I am a kinaesthetic learner!'

How would you respond to pupils who use their understanding of learning styles as an excuse for *not* engaging in an activity?

Learning styles, personalized learning and Assessment for Learning

Focusing on learning styles recognizes the unique qualities that individual pupils bring to the learning situation. This is referred to as the **personalized learning** approach. Advocates of personalized learning take a structured and responsive approach to each pupil in order that their students may be able to progress, achieve and participate. Central to personalized learning is the concept of Assessment for Learning (AfL) and effective teaching.

Assessment for Learning involves pupils and teachers together discussing where pupils are in the learning process, where they need to go next, and how best to get there (ARG 2002). The argument for AfL is that it can raise standards for all pupils and especially for pupils who have special educational needs. But what does Assessment for Learning look like? Well, in a classroom that uses this approach:

• Individual learning goals for the pupils and learning objectives (relating to the lesson) will be explained to all pupils so that all pupils know what they are working towards.

• Feedback from all those involved in supporting teaching and learning should relate to both the pupils' own learning goals and the learning objectives for the lesson. Feedback can be verbal or written but needs to inform the pupil of their successes and what they need to do to improve. Pupils need to be aware of not only what they need to learn but importantly how they need to go about this learning.

• Importantly, time must be made for this feedback and the feedback needs to be constructive and sensitive. Constructive feedback should motivate the pupil to learn.

• The teacher or teaching assistant and the pupil need to be involved in reviewing and reflecting on the learning that has occurred, and this should take place within everyday classroom practice.

• Pupils need to be taught how to assess their own learning so they are active in the learning process. Through AfL it is hoped that pupils will learn to take responsibility for their own learning and that eventually they will become independent learners. (ARG 2002)

In Assessment for Learning there are links to Vygotsky's concept of the Zone of Proximal Development, where a pupil's abilities can be described in terms of what they can achieve by themselves and what they can achieve with support. Once a pupil's abilities are known, constructive feedback can be given to promote further learning. (For further information on constructive feedback, see pages 70–1.) Central to the process of Assessment for Learning is that the pupil is made aware of what is required to learn and that they are active in this process.

Thinking deeply

What is personalized learning? Is it . . .
Looking at and valuing the individual child?
Explain your answer.
How do you do this?
Seeing the potential in every pupil and enabling the pupil to achieve their potential?
Explain your answer.
How do you do this?
Developing the whole child, academically, socially, emotionally, spiritually?
Explain your answer.
How do you do this?
Giving pupils ownership over their learning process?
Explain your answer.
How do you do this?

Case study 3.3

Reflecting on a lesson in a special school

Judy works at a school for children with mild and moderate learning disabilities. She works as a teaching assistant supporting children in developing life skills.

Description of what happened or should have happened
Today I was working in the kitchen supporting pupils learning about food technology. Today's task was for the pupils to make sausage rolls. I told the pupils what the learning objectives were and what they would need to do to accomplish this.

I told them that they would need to use the food processor to make the pastry. After the pupils had weighed the ingredients we read through the recipe together. I explained that the flour needed to be processed for about five seconds. I then told the pupils that the margarine should be cut into small pieces, added to the flour and processed for about ten seconds. I showed the pupils ten seconds on the timer. I explained that water should then be added a few drops at a time and the mixture should be processed until it became a ball of pastry in the bowl. I checked that the pupils understood the instructions by having them repeat them back to me. They both did this with some help and then they went back to their respective kitchens with a copy of the instructions.

Now, of the two pupils I was working with, Sidney has problems with reading and sometimes he has problems with anger management. The other pupil, Joe, has mild learning disabilities but is quite good at reading. I thought that of the two, Sidney would have the most problems in following the recipe, so I stayed with him and watched to make sure he carried out the instructions. Contrary to what I expected, he actually did very well and achieved the required result of a good ball of pastry.

I then moved on to the second pupil, Joe (the very able reader). Upon looking in his bowl, I realized that he had not followed the instructions but had combined all his ingredients together with too much water. Joe seemed very upset and said he hated cooking. I told him not to worry because the problem could be put right by adding some more flour before rolling out the pastry. In the end the sausage rolls were cooked and thoroughly enjoyed by both boys.

Feelings (What did I feel? How do I think the pupils felt?)
In the end we got there and I think the pupils enjoyed the activity. However, Joe was quite upset with the state of his pastry. In trying to set learning goals for next time, I asked Joe what he could do differently. Joe's response was, 'I don't know – you tell me!'

Evaluation (What was good? What was difficult?)
The pupils were involved in the learning. This was very much a hands-on activity, what Piaget would see as discovery learning. I feel I did not keep an adequate eye on both boys. I did, however, learn from this experience that while Joe is very good at reading he does not have the ability to use his reading skills to help him follow instructions.

Analysis (How do I make sense of this? Why did this happen?)
Well, from what I know about learning styles I would say that Joe could prefer to have frequent adult supervision.

In conclusion (What else could I have done?)
I could have stayed with Joe and let Sidney work by himself, or perhaps I could have worked with them both together.

Action plan (Next time I would . . .)
Next time I need to give more attention to Joe.

Thinking deeply

How would you describe Joe's and Sidney's learning styles?

What other possible explanations could there be for Joe's difficulties in the kitchen?

As a TA, what high quality constructive feedback would you give Joe and Sidney to promote their learning further?

What would you say to Joe and Sidney to help them set targets for future learning?

In helping pupils set targets for future learning, how do you respond to the pupil who says, 'I don't know – you tell me!'?

Chapter 4

Pupils with additional needs

Inclusion

Before beginning a chapter on pupils with additional needs it is essential to discuss the principle of inclusion. Inclusion is one of the main driving forces behind education. Inclusion starts with the individual pupil and sets out to remove barriers to learning by adapting teaching strategies in order to meet the pupil's individual needs. Inclusive practice:

- aims to ensure that all pupils have access to high quality education
- involves having high expectations for all pupils
- values all pupils; encourages all pupils to reach their potential and celebrates achievements, and
- aims to break down barriers by encouraging respectful relationships between pupils.

Inclusion is an ongoing process that engages all staff involved in supporting teaching and learning.

Terminology

While recognizing the individuality of pupils, there are a range of terms used to describe specific shared patterns of needs.

Children with additional needs

This is a broad term that describes pupils who are at risk of not achieving or achieving poor outcomes in relation to the government's *Every Child Matters* agenda (DfES 2004). Children with additional needs are said to be experiencing challenges to being healthy, staying safe, enjoying and achieving, making a positive contribution and achieving economic well-being. It is estimated that 20–30 per cent of pupils will be designated as having additional needs at some point during their school career and will therefore require support (DfCSF website 2010). As stated, 'children with additional needs' is a broad term and would cover children who are designated as having special education needs, those with mental health issues and those whose needs have not been formally identified but who are deemed to be at risk.

Children with special educational needs

This term is defined by the Education Act 1996 (Section 312) as referring to pupils who:

- have a significantly greater difficulty in learning than the majority of children of the same age, or
- have a disability that prevents or hinders them from making use of educational facilities of a kind generally provided for children of the same age, or
- are under compulsory school age and would be likely to fall within one of the above definitions if special provision was not made for them.

Again this definition is very broad and will include children who have been diagnosed as having **dyslexia**, **dyspraxia**, **ASC**, **ADHD**, communication disorders, **Down's syndrome** or physical/sensory impairments. However, even if two children have the same diagnosis, the degree or extent to which they have the condition will often differ.

A further complication is that often a child will have not one but a combination of conditions. When a child has a combination of conditions, experts talk about **co-morbidity**, i.e. the degree to which one condition is associated with another. For example, a child might have a dual diagnosis of dyslexia and ADHD with some of the tendencies of autism. **Tendencies** is a term used by experts when a child will have some aspects of that condition but not enough to warrant a diagnosis.

Vulnerable children

This term is used to describe children who are seen to be disadvantaged and who would benefit from extra help in order to make the best of their life chances. It is thought that children are unlikely to be vulnerable throughout their entire childhood, but may experience times of vulnerability due to impoverished home circumstances or special educational and health needs that impact on their ability to be part of a greater community and consequently results in them being at risk of being socially excluded.

We have covered numerous terms and of course these terms evolve and change with time. What is essential to remember when using terminology such as additional needs, autism or dyspraxia, is that terms are seen as a useful way of communicating shared patterns of need rather than being seen as labels that could lead to individuals being perceived in a negative manner and discriminated against.

In any discussion of additional needs it is also important to remember that a child is first and foremost an individual with his or her own personality. What all of this means for adults supporting children with additional needs is that every child is unique and will have their own distinctive profile of gifts, strengths and weaknesses. This awareness needs to be considered when looking at recommended teaching and learning support strategies. It would be nice to be able to say that if a child has dyslexia or autism, then just try this approach and they will learn. However, for the reasons already listed, it is not always that simple. A strategy that will work with one child might not work equally well with another child even though the two children have the same condition.

This chapter aims to describe briefly various additional needs and corresponding learning support and teaching strategies that have been found to be effective. When you are working with pupils with additional needs, as a teaching assistant you will very much be working under the direction of the teacher and the Special Educational Needs Coordinator (SENCO). Therefore, communication and dialogue between all those involved is crucial. To monitor the progress of a pupil, records need to be kept regarding what strategies have been tried and to what success. As a teaching assistant, your detailed observations and comments regarding what happens during a learning support session will be an important contribution to these records.

Assessing additional needs

Intelligence tests

A pupil's IQ or **intelligence test score** can be used as part of the process of diagnosing specific educational needs. Table 4.1 shows the relationship between the educational label and a pupil's IQ score (Atkinson *et al.* 1993).

Table 4.1 The relationship between educational labels and intelligence
scores

Educational label	IQ score
Very superior	130+
Superior	120–9
High average	110–19
Average	90–109
Low average	80–9
Borderline	70–9
Mild learning disabilities	55–69
Moderate learning disabilities	40–54
Severe learning disabilities	25–39
Profound learning disabilities	0–24

Educational psychologists will often use Wechsler Intelligence Scale for
Children (WISC-IV) to measure IQ. The current version (WISC-IV) is
comprised of a series of subtests to include verbal comprehension, perceptual reasoning, processing speed and working memory (see pages 144–5).
By comparing a pupil's overall IQ score with their individual scores on
various subtests, a profile of the pupil's strengths and weaknesses is revealed.
A profile can indicate what strategies need to be implemented to support
the pupil's learning. Let us look at a profile to discover what it can tell an
educational psychologist.

Case study 4.1

An IQ profile for Leon (10 years old)

Scale	Composite score	Qualitative description
Verbal comprehension	98	Average
Perceptual reasoning	102	Average
Working memory	68	Extremely low
Processing speed	106	Average
Full scale IQ	92	Average

This profile would tell an educational psychologist that although Leon's
verbal comprehension, perceptual reasoning and perceptual speed are within
the normal range, his working memory is very weak. Pupils with poor
working memory will typically have difficulties in following instructions,
make slow progress in reading and maths, appear to be inattentive, have

a short attention span, and be easily distracted (Gathercole and Alloway 2008). Once a weakness in working memory has been identified, specialized training programmes can be implemented. (For further information on working memory, see pages 144–5.)

Dynamic Assessment

Traditional tests given to pupils often measure unaided success or failure, i.e. how much pupils can or cannot do by themselves. However, recalling Vygotsky's Zone of Proximal Development (see page 19) we realize that there is a difference between unaided success and failure in terms of how much help or support the pupil requires in order to complete the task. Dynamic Assessment explores the amount and nature of support that the pupil needs to complete a task, and is said to provide an index of a pupil's readiness to change and learn. As such, this index can be used to explore differences between low-ability pupils (Fuchs *et al.* 2007). In case study 4.2, Sian, a teaching assistant at a special school, explains how she saw these differences.

Case study 4.2

Differences in responding to support

I was working with a group of pupils who were all having difficulties with basic addition. I was trying to explain to them how to use the technique of counting on with their fingers. Most of the pupils struggled with this, except Sam who immediately got it. It is funny how before I would say that they all were at the same level – but now I realize that pupils who seem to be at the same level actually differ in their ability to respond to support. My teacher was very interested in this observation.

Psychologists or psychiatrists use the *DSM* IV-TR (APA 2000) to establish whether an individual meets the criteria for a diagnosis. A diagnosis is important and useful as it communicates a shared pattern of need. However, it has been argued that the word diagnosis has negative connotations in that it implies that the condition is an illness, and that the condition could be cured and the patient needs to wait for the correct intervention or medication. In applying diagnoses to individuals, we need to recognize the role of the environment. One view of disability sees it as a social construction in that individuals are limited by barriers within the environment, specifically how others see them and how they view themselves. Changes in the environment and perceptions can therefore make a real difference to individuals. Language is important as it communicates how an individual is valued and perceived by society.

Thinking deeply

Of the phrases listed below, what phrases reflect the language of inclusion and why?

- label tins not people
- individuals with autism
- autistic individuals
- people first
- in handling children with autism

Can you give any examples of phrases that reflect the language of inclusion?

Autism Spectrum Conditions and Asperger's syndrome

Today psychologists and psychiatrists use two classification systems in order to determine whether someone has autism or Asperger's syndrome. The

Figure 9 Do not get into the situation where you can't see the pupil for the labels.

classification systems are the *Diagnostic and Statistical Manual* (*DSM* IV-TR, APA 2000) and the *International Classification of Diseases* (*ICD*, WHO 2007). These classification systems set out the behaviour an individual has to show in order to receive a certain diagnosis.

The difference between autism and Asperger's has been widely debated. Some will argue that Asperger's is the more able end of the autism spectrum, while others will argue that it is a very different condition. The *DSM* IV states that in contrast to autism, there are no clinically significant delays in language communication and cognitive development with Asperger's syndrome (APA 1995: 78).

When referring to autism and Asperger's syndrome, many professionals will use the phrase **Autism Spectrum Conditions**, or ASC for short. This phrase reflects the fact that individuals diagnosed with this condition will differ greatly in terms of ability. At one end of the spectrum you will have an individual with no language and profound learning disabilities, while at the other end the individual will have an average IQ and a good command of language.

So far, ASC has been described in the technical language used by psychologists and psychiatrists. However, what do these diagnostic criteria mean in practice? What are the characteristics or challenges a pupil with autism or Asperger's might show that a teacher or teaching assistant might notice? (But remember, individuals will differ in regard to the characteristics they demonstrate.)

Difficulties in social interaction

- The child might be reluctant to maintain eye contact.
- The child might have difficulty in making sense of, or understanding, body language and facial expressions.
- The child might have difficulty in developing age-appropriate friendships.
- The child will lack empathy. They will have difficulty in interpreting or responding to another person's emotional reactions. For example, if a child with ASC accidentally pushes another child over, he or she will not necessarily understand why the other child is upset or angry with them.
- The child will not realize that just as they have their own unique thoughts and feelings, so do other people; they lack a theory of mind (see page 35–6).
- The child will be confused by social situations.

Difficulties in communication and imaginative activity

- A child could have no language or be delayed in language development. The child does not try to make up for difficulties in language development by the use of facial expressions and body language.
- If the child does have language, there could be difficulties in starting and sustaining conversations. Such conversations will often break social rules (e.g. a pupil might ask the Head Teacher why his breath smells).
- A child might use repetitive phrases (e.g. jingle bells) that they have learned from others or from watching television. The key point here is that these phrases are not used to communicate with others but are spoken because the child simply likes the sound of the phrase.
- A child might have a wide vocabulary but have a tendency to take things literally. For example, if someone says it is raining cats and dogs, then the child might be looking to see where the cats and dogs are.
- There is a lack of spontaneous make-believe play. Children with ASC do not usually play with toys in a conventional manner. Children with ASC will often line toys up, and sometimes they can become fixated on one toy or object.

Figure 10 Alex had a tendency to take things literally.

Limited range of activities and interests

- An individual may have an all-consuming preoccupation with one or more restricted areas of interest, and this preoccupation is abnormal in its intensity or focus. Many individuals have hobbies, but in individuals with ASC the hobby or interest can become an obsession. For example, a small boy who becomes fascinated with vacuum cleaners, knows everything there is to know about vacuum cleaners and will, if given a chance, talk about nothing else but vacuum cleaners.
- Keeping to routines or rituals is extremely important for children with ASC. If routines are broken, this will lead to great distress. For example, the child might insist: 'At 10:45 we go out for our break. We can't go out for break at 10:30 as it is not the right time. The right time is 10:45.'
- An individual may exhibit repetitive motor mannerisms. This can take the form of hand-flapping, clapping or rocking backwards and forwards.

In addition there may be differences in regard to sensory perceptions. Some individuals with ASC will be hypersensitive to certain sounds, smells, lights and textures. Furthermore, some individuals may have very high pain thresholds.

Strategies for dealing with these challenges

Lack of eye contact

Do not expect eye contact and never turn their face to look at you (*Special Children*, 2001b: 37).

Obsession with routines

A structured environment with specific areas for specific tasks and an area for individual work and personal space is recommended. Treatment and Education of Autistic and related Communications-handicapped Children (TEACCH) is widely used within schools. The TEACCH approach (Mesibov 2003) talks about the culture of autism and the need for structure. Structure is important to an individual with autism as change is seen as frightening. A rigid routine will allow the pupil with autism to be able to predict to a certain extent what is going to happen next. If a pupil feels secure in the routine, then hopefully they will begin to feel comfortable and relaxed. At this stage they will then be able to learn. If a child with autism has difficulties in communication, it is suggested that routines be indicated by visual aids. One aid could be the use of a visual timetable, which is constantly available to the child. If a child has not developed the ability to tell the time by looking at a watch or a clock, a large adapted hourglass or egg-timer could be used to indicate to the child when it is time to move on to the next activity.

Lack of understanding of how to react in social situations

The *social story* approach developed by Carol Gray (1994) aims to describe a situation which the child finds personally difficult. As this approach focuses on the telling of a story, it is designed for the more able child with ASC. It is important that the story is written in a language that matches the child's level of understanding. There are formulas for writing such stories. These include:

- *Descriptive sentences.* These sentences describe exactly what happens, where it happens and why it happens. The reasons for participating in the activity are given. In day-to-day life there are many unwritten and unspoken rules regarding social expectations and codes of behaviour. These unwritten and unspoken rules need to be specifically pointed out and explained to a child with ASC. These descriptive sentences should include terms such as 'usually' or 'sometimes' rather than 'always'. The use of such words will help a child with ASC deal with unexpected changes to the routines.
- *Perspective sentences.* These sentences describe the responses, reactions and feelings of other people in a situation. A child with ASC will not understand why other people do what they do and in this respect will benefit from such information.
- *Directive sentences.* These sentences often take the form of gentle advice. For example: 'I will try to do this' (Rowe 1999; Smith 2001).

Case study 4.3

A social story

Jason finds sitting in the school assembly difficult. When the other children talk and shout, Jason becomes visibly upset and screams at them to be quiet. Sometimes Jason becomes so angry, he has to be removed from the assembly. The SENCO at Jason's school has suggested he write about going to assembly. Here is Jason's story:

> My name is Jason.
> I am a pupil at Crossroads village school.
> A lot of other boys and girls go to our school.
> Usually Mrs Robinson teaches my class and Miss Philips helps me with my work.
> Usually the whole school goes to assembly every morning.
> Usually we go to assembly after the teacher has taken the register.
> When we are in assembly we are supposed to sit quietly.
> Sometimes children can be very noisy. Sometimes children can make a lot of noise moving their chairs.
> When the other children make noise it is up to the teachers and other helpers to ask them to be quiet.
> I will try to ignore the noise the other children are making.
> I should try to sit quietly in assembly.
> If I sit quietly everyone will be very pleased with me.
> My teachers will all say, 'Isn't Jason good?' 'Jason is a good boy for behaving so well in assembly.'

Dyslexia

Individuals with dyslexia will have difficulties with words. **Dyslexia** has been defined as a:

> specific learning disability that is neurobiological in origin. It is characterized by difficulties with accurate and or fluent word recognition and by poor spelling and decoding abilities. These difficulties typically result from a deficit in the phonological component of language that is often unexpected in relation to other cognitive abilities and the provision of effective classroom instruction.
>
> (Lyon, Shaywitz and Shaywitz 2003: 2)

Therefore, in order to diagnose dyslexia, an educational psychologist must rule out:

- overall low intelligence
- lack of schooling
- a socially disadvantaged background that did not provide the child with opportunities to read and enjoy books

- hearing or visual difficulties, and
- emotional or behavioural difficulties that might influence the child's ability to learn.

Not surprisingly, it often takes time for dyslexia to be diagnosed. Dyslexia is seen as a discrepancy between the child's general ability and the child's performance on reading and spelling tests. What teachers or teaching assistants will notice is that an apparently very bright child is just not progressing at reading and spelling.

The sort of challenges that might occur and what a teacher or teaching assistant might notice

Poor auditory short-term memory

- Inability to carry out a sequence of instructions.
- Forgetting what he or she was going to say in the middle of a sentence or a conversation.
- Difficulties in remembering what was given for homework.

Difficulties in language and speech

- Late speech development.
- Confusion between similar sounds in speech, e.g. 'f', 'th' and 'v'.
- Inability to recognize rhymes.

Difficulties with visual processing

- Difficulties in coordinating binocular vision, which results in the child feeling that the words on the page are moving.
- Oversensitivity to light or glare, which would make reading difficult.

Difficulties in sequencing and organizing

- Difficulty in learning the days of the week, months of the year.
- Difficulty in organizing ideas.
- Difficulty in organizing notes for study and revision.

Difficulties in phonological awareness

- Inability to remember sound/letter (symbol) associations, i.e. what sounds go with which letters.
- Difficulty in blending letter sounds together to form words.
- Bizarre spelling, as a result of not knowing which letters correspond to which sounds.

Overreliance on phonics

Not all individuals with dyslexia will have the same pattern of difficulties. Some individuals seem to understand sound/letter associations but tend to make errors in treating *irregular* words as *regular* words. For example a pupil might read 'island' as 'izland' or they might spell 'island' as 'iland'.

Poor sense of direction

Dyslexics may confuse their left and right, or up and down.

Clumsiness

Individuals who have dyslexia have a higher risk of also having dyspraxia (*Special Children* 2000c; Pascal 2002).

It is important to note that pupils with dyslexia will differ in regard to the severity of their condition and the reasons underlying their difficulties. For example, some pupils might struggle with reading and spelling because of their difficulties with visual processing, whereas others are struggling because of difficulties with phonological awareness or perhaps an overreliance on phonics. The fact that dyslexia has a number of causes is important because the teaching and learning support strategy needs to take into account the reasons for the pupils' difficulties.

How to deal with these challenges

It is helpful to note that the following strategies are useful for both pupils who have been diagnosed with dyslexia and other pupils who are experiencing difficulties with reading and spelling.

Multi-sensory techniques

Multi-sensory techniques involve the teaching of phonics through an approach that uses all senses, i.e. auditory, visual, and kinaesthetic and tactile (Thomson 1990). For example, a pupil would be taught through the following approaches.

- *Auditory.* The pupil hears the word and would be required to repeat the word.
- *Visual.* The pupil sees the printed word. Sometimes pupils can look in a mirror when reading words so they can see how their lips and tongue form the sounds. Sometimes pupils can be encouraged to see or visualize the word on the wall and then copy it down.
- *Kinaesthetic and tactile.* The pupil writes the word. Using joined-up writing is helpful as it encourages the hand to remember the sequence of movements. Sometimes the pupils are encouraged to feel the word as it is presented to them in three-dimensional letters. Alternatively pupils could trace the letters in the sand or on someone's back. Running around big shapes and letters in the playground establishes a whole-body feel for the shapes involved (BBC 1997; Pascal 2002).

Memory techniques

Hardwick (1996) suggests using personalized flashcards to help pupils remember words they find difficult. On one side of the flashcard the pupil writes the word; on the other side they write a personally meaningful sentence including that word. For example, on one side of the flashcard is the target word 'believe' and on the other side is written: 'I want to believe' accompanied by a picture of a UFO. Or imagine the target word is 'never': on one side is the word 'never' and on the other side is written 'you will never make me talk' with an accompanying picture of a spy.

Pupils can also make up stories to help remember words that they find difficult; for example, 'Sister Alice is dizzy' stands for 'said'.

Structured programmes

There are many programmes that exist to teach the skills involved in reading and spelling. Some programmes concentrate on a phonics approach, i.e. learning systematically the rules associating letters with sounds. Other programmes focus on more visual approaches such as encouraging the pupil to recognize words within words. For example 'damage' is composed of two words, 'dam' and 'age'. Regardless of what teaching/learning support strategy is used with the pupil, a key role of the teaching assistant working with such a pupil would be to pay close attention to how the pupil progresses and to record this information. Important information to record would include not only what words the pupil got *right*, but also what words they got *wrong*. It is important to record how the pupil writes the word because an analysis of spelling mistakes might reveal clues to underlying difficulties.

Thinking deeply

What specific programmes and strategies does your school use to support and teach pupils who have dyslexia?

In your opinion, how effective are these programmes and strategies?

Case study 4.4

Working with a pupil who has difficulty reading

Valerie, a teaching assistant in a Year 3 class, was working with Sonia. Sonia, though a bright young child, struggled with reading and spelling. Valerie was reading a book entitled *Biff and Chip go to the Moon*. Sonia had been on the same book for the last two days but was still having difficulty with most of the words. Sonia struggled through the first two pages and then said that she was fed up with the book and that she wasn't going to read any more.

On a very practical level there are certain things that Valerie could do to help Sonia with her reading. Pascal (2002) recommends:

- If a child is having great difficulty sounding out a word, step in and give a suitable prompt to the pupil. For example, if the pupil got stuck on the word 'climb', say the first part of the word, i.e. 'cli', then if necessary complete the word. The key point is not to let frustration build up.
- Share the reading. You, the teaching assistant, read one line, the pupil can read the next. Sometimes using funny voices can help motivate younger pupils.
- Every now and then stop and talk about what has happened and what you think will happen next. This encourages comprehension. Perhaps the pupil can use these clues about what should happen next to help him or her sound out the words.

• Perhaps, as a break from reading the required text on the reading scheme, the pupil can read a book of their own choice. The key point is that the activity of reading is enjoyable.

Thinking deeply

When working with pupils who have difficulties reading it is important to consider the role of motivation. Low motivation to read may result from a pupil fearing that they will fail and therefore they are doing everything that they can to try and avoid a difficult and painful task.

How do you encourage pupils with low motivation to read (and high motivation to avoid failing) to have a go?

Dyspraxia

Dyspraxia, or **Developmental Coordination Disorder** (as it is called in the *DSM* IV-TR), is when a child experiences difficulties in motor coordination that cannot be explained by a general medical condition and these difficulties result in the child being substantially behind their peers in motor milestones. Dyspraxia has also been referred to as motor learning difficulty, perceptuo motor dysfunction, and deficits in attention motor control and perception (DAMP). Difficulties in motor coordination can affect both gross and fine motor skills. In some individuals the motor movements affected also include the mouth and the tongue, resulting in difficulties with speech. This is termed verbal dyspraxia or apraxia of speech. These difficulties in motor coordination are thought to result from an immaturity in the way in which the brain processes information.

Conrad *et al.* (1983) talk of two aspects of dyspraxia: **ideational** dyspraxia and **ideo-motor** dyspraxia.

• *Ideational dyspraxia* refers to difficulties with planning a sequence of coordinated movements. These children might always put their socks and shoes on before their trousers.

• *Ideo-motor dyspraxia* refers to individuals who know what they want to do, know what the right sequence of actions is, but somehow their body does not do what they want it to. These individuals appear awkward and clumsy.

The sort of challenges that might occur and what a teacher or teaching assistant might notice

Fine motor difficulties

- Messy handwriting; poor copying skills; immature drawings.
- Lack of secure tripod grip of pen or pencil.
- Difficulty in dressing; for example, struggles to fasten buttons and do up shoelaces; always the last to get changed in PE.
- Great difficulties in using scissors.
- Difficulties with assembling puzzles; avoids construction toys.
- Messy eaters.

Gross motor difficulties

- Poor posture; awkward movements.
- Poor PE skills: difficulties in running, hopping, climbing, balancing and catching or kicking a ball.

Poor spatial awareness

- Tendency to bump into objects or people.
- Tendency to drop objects or knock things over. Individuals seem to have difficulty in being aware of how close their hands are, or need to be, to objects.
- Tendency to get too close to others, to be 'right in your face'.

Poor auditory and visual short-term memory

- Poor listening skills.
- Difficulties in following sequential instructions. If given a series of three instructions such as 'Put your name on your work, put your work on my desk, and then put your chair on the table', the child with dyspraxia might put their chair on the table but in doing so forget the other two instructions.
- Difficulty in copying words from the board.

No laterality or lack of bilateral integration (i.e. inability to integrate both sides of the body)

- No clearly dominant hand. Sometimes they will write with their right hand and sometimes they will write with their left.

- The child will use the right hand to do tasks on the right side of their body and will use their left hand to do tasks on the left side of their body.

Organizational skills

- Poorly developed organizational skills. For example, has difficulty remembering what to bring to school, what homework needs to be completed, what class they should be in. This is especially a problem in secondary school.

Difficulties in social esteem

- All of these difficulties can lead to the individual being isolated, friendless and ridiculed (*Special Children* 2000a; Ripley *et al.* 1997).

How to deal with these challenges

The first point to make is that those children who are dyspraxic need to be recognized as such and not just labelled as awkward or clumsy.

It is suggested that programmes of activities which focus on gross and fine motor movements be practised on a daily basis. These programmes often include practising a good upright posture, balance, jumping, and finger exercises and cross lateral exercises, such as touching the right knee with the left hand. Such exercises are developed on an individual basis with input from physiotherapists. Often teaching assistants are involved in implementing such programmes.

Aside from these programmes involving practising physical activities, there are a number of practical steps that can be taken to help the pupil with dyspraxia. Let us look at case study 4.5, which is written from a pupil's perspective.

Case study 4.5

John's story

I arrive late in class. I have forgotten my book bag again! Miss is cross. I can't sit down as I have no chair. I walk over to get one, but I fall over Tom's feet and in the process knock down the new science display! Miss is not pleased! Everyone laughs at me!

It is the literacy hour. Miss reads a story. But I find it hard to follow as I find it hard to keep still. Billy complains to the teacher that I keep bumping him. I don't do it on purpose, it just happens. After Miss has finished the story I go back to my seat and am told to copy the words from the board. I find this difficult! My pencil is broken and every time I sharpen it breaks again. Everyone on my table has finished copying the words and I haven't started. I have to stay in at break and finish copying the words.

After break it is time for numeracy. We are playing with the Mental Maths Monkey. James throws me the monkey and I am supposed to catch it and answer the question $2 + 2 = ?$ I am happy, as I know the answer, but I miss catching the monkey and it lands in the fish tank. When I try to get the monkey out of the fish tank, I catch a fish and hurt it. I didn't mean to.

It is lunchtime. No one wants to sit next to me as they say I make such a mess and that I look disgusting when I eat. I am not looking forward to the afternoon as we have PE.

What this case study illustrates is how difficult the school day can be for a pupil with dyspraxia. However, there are ways in which the day could be made easier. With knowledge of the kind of things that John finds difficult, the teacher and teaching assistant could make the day easier. A teaching assistant could ensure that John has a seat that he can easily get to when he arrives in the class. A teaching assistant could be on hand to provide John with some pencils that have already been sharpened. The teacher could write on the board with different coloured pens for every line. Alternatively, John could have a copy of the words beside him. John could be given extra time to complete his work or be given a target that he can achieve; for example, a certain number of words. It is important that John not be put in situations where he will fail. Instead of throwing the Mental Maths Monkey, the monkey could be passed around. Most important, John needs praise and lots of praise to boost his self-esteem.

Down's syndrome

In 1959 Down's syndrome was identified as a chromosomal disorder: instead of there being forty-six chromosomes in each cell, there are forty-seven. Later the extra chromosome was identified as a partial or an extra chromosome 21; thus sometimes Down's syndrome is referred to as Trisomy 21. While there are common traits similar to all individuals with Down's syndrome, there are also great variations in terms of ability between individuals.

The sort of challenges that might occur and what a teacher or teaching assistant might notice

Hearing

• Figures suggest that as many as 40 per cent of individuals with Down's syndrome have mild hearing loss, with 15 per cent having severe hearing loss. Hearing tests are essential for individuals with Down's syndrome.

Limited auditory short-term memory

• Difficulty listening to and following complex instructions.

• Might repeat the last part of what you have said to them – because this might be the only part of the sentence that they have heard and remembered. In this case, you might need to repeat all of what you have just said.

Thinking, reasoning and generalizing knowledge to new situations

• An individual might learn how to add 20 + 5 but have difficulties generalizing that skill so that they can add a different sum.

Delayed motor skills, fine and gross

• As in dyspraxia, there could be difficulties with fine movement, e.g. handwriting, using eating utensils or doing up buttons, and with gross skills such as running and jumping.

Difficulties in speech production

• What is said can be hard to understand due to difficulties in pronunciation.

Past difficulties with low expectations

In the past, society has assumed that individuals with Down's syndrome have limited capabilities. Up to 1979 it was the opinion of professionals that individuals with Down's syndrome were incapable of learning to read, and therefore they were never taught. However, research has revealed that with the right teaching approach, many Down's syndrome children can learn to read (Buckley and Bird 1993; Buckley 1995; *Special Children* 2001a). Indeed, the ability to read is now considered a strength within the learning profile of children with Down's syndrome. In terms of teaching reading skills a 'whole word approach' has proven to be very successful. Such reading schemes build on a sight vocabulary of key functional and common words. The use of such reading schemes are based on the fact that in individuals with Down's syndrome, the visual memory may be more effective than the auditory memory. Furthermore, although individuals with Down's syndrome might have difficulty expressing themselves through spoken communication, they are often very good at picking up and interpreting body language and facial expressions and making their feelings and thoughts known through non-verbal communication.

How to deal with these challenges

The publication *Special Children* (2001a) recommends to:

- Keep instructions short and simple. If instructions are too long, an individual with a limited short-term memory will only remember a small part of what is said.
- Use familiar language. Always check for understanding before proceeding with a task.
- Make the most of visual material when teaching new skills.
- Listen carefully, because individuals with Down's syndrome often have difficulty in speech pronunciation.
- Set realistic targets.
- Have individuals with Down's syndrome practise fine and gross motor skills.

Case study 4.6

Working with a pupil who has Down's syndrome

Amy was working with John, a Year 7 pupil with Down's syndrome. Recently Amy had attended a training day on supporting pupils with Down's syndrome. Amy decided to use her newly acquired knowledge to help her plan a learning support session with John on the recognition of money. This is what Amy planned to do:

- Lay real coins on a table (50p, 20p, 10p and 5p).
- Point to the coins and ask John what they were.
- Ask John to select a certain coin and state what it was.
- Once confident with the task, move the lesson to the vending machine in the cafeteria.
- Let John choose an item that he wished to have. He then needed to select the correct money and decide which coin went into which slot. If John was correct he could keep the chosen item as a reward.

Amy reported that the lesson went very well and led to John having greater confidence with money both inside and outside of school.

ADHD

The *DSM* IV-TR (APA 2000) describes three types of attention disorder:

1. Attention Deficit/Hyperactivity Disorder, predominantly inattentive
2. Attention Deficit/Hyperactivity Disorder, predominantly hyperactive-impulsive
3. Attention Deficit/Hyperactivity Disorder, combined.

Most children will have times when they find it difficult to pay attention, or they are overactive or they act without thinking. But what marks individuals with this disorder as different from your average child is the degree to which they have difficulties in these areas and how these difficulties influence all aspects of their lives.

The sort of challenges that might occur and what a teacher or teaching assistant might notice

Inattention

- Makes careless mistakes in schoolwork, often as a result of not paying close attention to detail.
- Has difficulty staying on task.
- Often does not listen when spoken to.
- Often fails to complete an activity.
- Has difficulties with organization. Often loses things and forgets to bring the right equipment to class.
- Is easily distracted.

Hyperactivity

- Can't keep still; constantly fidgeting.
- Constantly leaves seat to move around, even though instructed to remain seated.
- Runs or climbs excessively in situations which are inappropriate.
- Finds it difficult to participate in quiet pastimes.
- Talks constantly.

Impulsiveness

- Blurts out answers without waiting to be asked.
- Acts without considering the consequences; acts first, thinks later.
- Has difficulty in awaiting turns.
- Interrupts conversations or games.

Difficulties in relating to others

- Peers may find children with ADHD difficult to relate to and not want to play with them. Challenges children with ADHD face in relating to others are often a consequence of being impulsive and hyperactive.

Difficulties in self-esteem

- Because the child with ADHD finds it difficult to pay attention and stay on task, they will often fall behind their peers academically. Difficulties with attention, hyperactivity and impulsiveness will often mean that these children are in trouble with the teacher. This combined with difficulties in relating to other children can lead to poor self-esteem and behavioural difficulties (*Special Children* 2000b; APA 1995).

How to deal with these challenges

Medication

Although this remains a controversial and emotional issue, treating ADHD children with stimulant medication can have beneficial results. Psychostimulants, such as Ritalin (methylphenidate), have been found to improve attention span and impulse control and to decrease incidences of hyperactivity in 70–90 per cent of children with ADHD (Barkley 1998). However, other findings indicate that a combination of medication and behavioural strategies are most effective for enhancing behaviour and well-being in social, family and school settings (Conners *et al.* 2001).

If you are supporting a pupil who has been prescribed medication for ADHD, it is important to find out as much as possible about the medication. For example, you should know that Ritalin is a short-acting medication and multiple dosages need to be given. It starts to work in about twenty to forty minutes with maximum effectiveness occurring after an hour and a half, and it starts to wear off after four hours. If the dosage is not correct then a condition called rebound hyperactivity could occur. What this means is that when the Ritalin starts to wear off, the pupil becomes even more hyperactive than they ever were before taking the Ritalin. If a teacher or teaching assistant notices this, then the pupil's doctor needs to be informed and the dosage corrected.

A specially designed environment: the ADHD classroom

Pupils with ADHD benefit from a highly structured environment and clear boundaries. Such children will find it difficult to cope in an open classroom where there are lots of distractions. Detweiler *et al.* (1995) see an ideal classroom as having the following characteristics:

- A small classroom with one teacher, one teaching assistant and ten children.
- A room with four walls, windows above the eye level of pupils (so the pupils can't look out) and absolutely no open space leading to other classrooms.
- A set routine with no changing of teaching and ensuring that subjects are taught in the same order every day.
- Daily programmes and weekly programmes on each pupil's desk.
- Separate study booths for individual work. Earphones can be used to block out background noise.

Case study 4.7

Strategies for pupils with additional needs can often be successful with all pupils

Laure worked as a TA in a large secondary school, and supported many pupils with ADHD. Often she would use daily programmes and weekly programmes as visual reminders. When Laure was working with the PE pupils on the field, she noticed that they would often lose focus all together and just run around and muck about. Laure suggested to the teacher that they could use a visual reminder. So now Laure and the teacher bring a moveable whiteboard out (weather permitting) and write the learning outcomes on the board. It is surprising how something so simple can make such a difference. Now when the pupils start to lose focus Laure or the teacher point to the board, or better still the pupils look at the board to remind themselves of what they should be doing

Table 4.2 Teaching ADHD pupils to self-monitor aspects of their academic behaviour

Task	What is taught?	Example: a pupil is working on a maths worksheet
To self-monitor performance	Pupil is taught to note, record, assess and evaluate aspects of their academic performance.	A pupil may be taught to note how many problems they attempted, how much time they spent on planning, how many problems they got correct, and to consider how they could do better.
To self-monitor attention	Pupil is taught to note, record, assess and evaluate their on-task behaviours.	A pupil may be taught to ask themselves at regular times whether they were paying attention. A pupil may be specifically asked to record on a tally sheet whether they are on-task every time the buzzer sounds.

Underachievement is common in pupils with ADHD. Research indicates this is not due to a lack of ability but from difficulties in self-monitoring or self-regulating behaviour (Harris *et al.* 2005). Therefore, Harris *et al.* (2005) recommend teaching pupils with ADHD how to self-monitor aspects of their performance and attention. But what does this mean in practice?

Case study 4.8

Working with a pupil who has ADHD

Tina worked as a teaching assistant in a mainstream secondary school. One of the pupils Tina supported was Wayne, a Year 7 pupil. Tina describes the following lesson with Wayne.

'It was Design and Technology. The class were working on designing juggling balls. I had worked hard with Wayne in coming up with a design for the juggling balls. In this class the pupils were to start work assembling their project. Each pupil had a sewing machine to work with. As well as working with and supporting Wayne, I also had to deal with other pupils' requests to help them set up their sewing machines. I tried to get Wayne started and then I went over to another pupil. Well, Wayne was all over the place. When I was with someone else, he was over at the other end of the room. Wayne is incredibly agile and at one point he vaulted over an empty desk. Wayne is incredibly good at gymnastics, but unfortunately in the process he knocked over the teacher's box of extra spools of thread. It took me five minutes to pick them all up and of course the teacher was not impressed with Wayne. Wayne was supposed to be helping me, but instead he was talking to a group of boys. In fact, he had his arms around a boy's neck. Wayne said he was just messing about but the other boy didn't look too happy. The lesson went very quickly and Wayne unfortunately did not accomplish much.

Obviously Wayne is hard to keep on task. What could the teaching assistant do to make things easier?

- Perhaps Wayne could be placed as near to the teacher as possible with his back to other pupils so he is not distracted by what others are doing. Alternatively, Wayne could be placed near pupils who regularly got on with their work, with these pupils serving as good role models.
- Perhaps the teaching assistant could have gone over with Wayne at the beginning of class exactly what he was expected to achieve within the class. The tasks set would need to be achievable, and the instructions would need to be clear and concise. The teaching assistant would need to check for understanding. Perhaps a written reminder of what he was supposed to do could be placed on his desk.
- The teaching assistant would need to observe Wayne closely and catch him when he is on task and then offer lots of praise.

Thinking deeply

Perhaps Wayne could be taught to self-monitor his performance and his attention to the task.

How would you do this?

Speech, language and communication difficulties

Communication is more than the spoken language; it refers to an individual's ability to understand what is happening around them and to be able to make their thoughts and wishes understood by others. Communication is central to the learning process and obviously children who have difficulties with communication will find learning difficult. Unresolved communication difficulties can lead to frustration and behaviour difficulties, and have a negative impact on self-esteem.

The sort of challenges that might occur and what a teacher or teaching assistant might notice

No verbal language by the age of three

As well as a lack of language, there might be no indication that the child understands what is said to them; nor does the child attempt to communicate with others. Possible reasons for such behaviour are deafness or other neurological disabilities.

Delayed language development

Though the child is developing language, their language at any given age will be more similar to a child who is very much younger. Often this delay is also evident in other areas such as social behaviour, motor skills and intellectual development. If all areas of development are affected then this would indicate global learning disabilities.

Case study 4.9

Delayed language development

Teaching assistant:	What did you do on the weekend?
Sarah (aged 8):	Swim! Big swim!
Teaching assistant:	Did you go swimming?
Sarah:	Yeah! Big swim!

Language is qualitatively impaired

Here the key feature is not one of delay but of difference. For example, suppose a child who has the ability to combine two or three words is asked to repeat the sentence 'Mummy is going to the shop.' A child displaying normal language development will say: 'Mummy going shop.' But a child whose understanding of language is qualitatively impaired might say: 'Is to going.' Clearly this child, though able to repeat three words, has not really understood what was meant by the sentence.

Difficulties in comprehension: echolalia

Often children who have difficulties in comprehension will also have a limited vocabulary. However, sometimes a child can exhibit what is called **echolalia**, which is the repeating of the language heard in others. Most children will do this at some times, but where this becomes an issue of concern is where the phrases are used without the purpose to communicate. Delayed echolalia is the repeating of phrases, hours, days or even weeks after the initial phrase was heard. This condition is common in the speech of some children with ASC.

Case study 4.10

An example of echolalia

Teaching assistant:	How many blocks do you have?
Young boy:	My giddy aunt!
Teaching assistant:	Where are the blocks?
Young boy:	My giddy aunt.

Difficulties in comprehension: hyperlexia

Hyperlexia is a condition where a child's reading skills greatly surpass their comprehension skills. For example, a child might fluently read 'The recovery of extraterrestrial saucers is important to UFO enthusiasts' yet have no idea what the sentence means. This condition is often associated with autism.

Difficulties in speaking (expressive language)

Some children have **difficulties articulating** words or certain sounds. They know what they want to say; it just does not come out the right way. Sometimes children will replace one consonant with another, e.g. 'wee-waw' for 'see-saw'. Difficulties in articulation can be explained by many factors including conditions such as cerebral palsy or cleft palate that affect the motor movements in speech. It is thought that difficulties in hearing due to repeated ear infections can also lead to some children having difficulties with articulation.

Stammering, sometimes referred to as stuttering, describes speech that is tense, hesitant and jerky. Signs may include:

- Blocks – getting so stuck on a word that no sound or only a strangled sound emerges.
- Sounds are prolonged, e.g. ssssssssaid.
- Repetitions of part of word or certain sounds, e.g. 'Pre-pre-pre-present, Miss'.
- The use of fillers, e.g. 'er', 'you know', 'like'.

A pupil who stammers might also show signs of physical tension and nervousness such as grimacing, blinking hard, avoiding eye contact, coughing and blushing. Some pupils may go to great lengths to avoid talking. A pupil's difficulties with stammering can vary from moment to moment, hour to hour and day to day (British Stammering Association 1997; Berko Gleason 1997).

How to deal with these challenges

The role of the audiologist and the speech and language therapist

An *audiologist* assesses an individual's ability to hear, while a *speech and language therapist* will evaluate the degree of communicative competence, i.e. the extent to which the child can communicate. A speech and language therapist could use a test from the Derbyshire Language scheme to measure comprehension level, i.e. how many words in a sentence a child understands.

Case study 4.11

A child with severely limited communication

Teaching assistant:	After lunch we are going to go swimming.
Child:	(runs and gets swimming gear)
Teaching assistant:	No, not now. After lunch!
Child:	(starts to yell and throws swimming gear on ground)

In case study 4.11, the child is functioning at just a one-word level. The child is only responding to one key word in the sentence – in this case, 'swimming'. The knowledge of how much a child understands can be used to enhance communication. If you know how many key words in a sentence a child can understand, then your language to the child will need to change to match their level of understanding. A speech and language therapist will offer advice in this area. A speech and language therapist will also work with pupils who have difficulties with articulation and suggest various strategies. Often teaching assistants will work with pupils using exercises that have been designed by the speech and language therapist.

Programmes such as Picture Exchange Communications

The Picture Exchange Communication System (Bondy and Frost 1994) was developed to encourage communication in young children with autism by creating a meaningful communicative environment, i.e. an environment where a pupil's attempts at communication are encouraged so that the pupil realizes that there is a connection between what they do (their attempts to communicate) and what happens to them (how others respond). The system is now used with all individuals who have difficulties communicating. In a sense this programme tries to teach those who have no communication the purpose of communication. There are a number of steps in this programme.

1. The child is observed and what they like, i.e. their preferences, are recorded. For example, one child may be very fond of apple slices at snack time while another child has an obsession with raisins.
2. Once preferences are established, pictures of the preferences are made into picture cards.
3. The child is then shown their preferred object and its corresponding picture. So in this example, they would be shown the slices of apple on a plate, and the picture of the slices of apple. After that, the child must give the trainer the picture if they want to get their slices of apple. To begin with, the child might need much encouragement and prompting.
4. Once the child has made the association between giving a picture card and receiving an object, more picture cards can be introduced.

In time children will be able to combine picture cards to form sentences. Individuals using this system will carry around a personalized book of picture cards (backed with Velcro), including a Velcro strip to which they add the picture cards to form sentences.

Recommendations from the British Stammering Society

Case study 4.12

Working with a child who stammers

Judy, the teaching assistant, and Mrs Rogers, the French teacher, were discussing Antonia, a bright Year 9 pupil who had a problem with stammering and who had just joined the class. Judy stated that Antonia had approached her at break and seemed very anxious about talking in class. Mrs Rogers said that she was also aware of Antonia's anxiety and had contacted a speech and language therapist. Mrs Rogers said the therapist had suggested the following, based on recommendations by the British Stammering Society (1997):

- Talk to Antonia and ask her what would make it easier for her. For example, perhaps at least to begin with, she could answer the register by raising her hand.
- Always maintain eye contact.
- Do not hurry her along or finish her words or sentences for her.
- Concentrate on what is being said, not how it is being said.
- Give Antonia the option of doing oral tests in private rather than in front of the class.
- Possibly, when practising French phrases in class, allow Antonia to work in a small group and have all pupils say the phrases together.
- Allow Antonia to be in a group of friends or supportive pupils so that she can avoid those children who might tease her.
- Most of all, give her lots of praise.

Sensory impairment

Generally there are two types of sensory impairment: visual and hearing.

The sort of challenges that might occur when supporting pupils with visual impairment and what a teacher or teaching assistant might notice

Difficulties with visual impairment

Different pupils will have varying levels of visual impairment. Pupils with no sight will need to be taught Braille or Moon (for further information on these tactile systems, see page 132), while others with some sight will need adaptations made to their environment or work materials so they can make the best use of the sight that they do have.

Difficulties with recognition

Some people can fail to recognize those they know. In order to recognize an object or person, the brain needs to store some representation of that object or person, so you can say: 'Why, that's Fred. I haven't seen him for ages' or 'That's an unusual-looking car.' Very rarely, the part of the brain that is responsible for these functions is damaged. Individuals who have difficulties with facial recognition are said to be suffering from a condition called **prosopagnosia**. Although these individuals have no difficulties with seeing, faces make no sense to them. Such individuals need to be taught alternative strategies for recognizing people.

Difficulties with orientation

In order to find our way around our environment, we need to have a visual memory of our environment stored in our mind. Obviously some people are better at remembering locations than others. Children who have severe difficulties in this regard will find that they get lost, even in familiar environments such as home and school. Additionally, these pupils will often have great difficulty in remembering where they have put things.

Difficulty in seeing parts of an image against a complex background

In this case the children will be able to see an object if it is on a plain background but would not be able to see the same object if it is placed on a patterned background.

Impaired depth perception

Children with difficulties in depth perception will find climbing up or down stairs or negotiating kerbs difficult. This is because when they see a line on the floor, they will not know whether it indicates a step or not. In trying to cope with such difficulties, such children tend to stop if they see a line on the ground, especially if the line is of a different colour, and test carefully with their feet to see if there is a step or not. However, such children will often trip over kerbs as the kerb and the road are often in the same colour. Occupational therapists can help children with this condition.

Impaired perception of movement

Children with this condition will find it difficult to see and understand fast-moving objects such as cars whizzing by them. Furthermore, children might find it difficult seeing what is around them if they are running. In addition, making sense of fast-moving television programmes can be difficult for these children.

The sort of challenges that might occur when supporting pupils with a hearing impairment and what a teacher or teaching assistant might notice

Individuals will differ in regard to how much they can hear. Some individuals will be totally deaf, while others will have some hearing. Sounds are invisible vibrations that travel in waves. Sounds differ in both loudness and pitch (frequency). *Frequency* or *pitch* refers to the speed at which the sound waves vibrate. Low frequency or low pitch refers to slow-moving sound waves, while high frequency or high pitch refers to fast-moving sound waves. For example, the sound of ocean waves is low in frequency, while the ring of a telephone is of a high frequency. Those children who have some hearing will need to be assessed to determine what sounds they can hear (Dutton 1997; National Deaf Children's Society 2001; Carter 1998).

How to deal with these challenges facing the sensory impaired

Braille and Moon

Braille and Moon are tactile systems of communication that are used by the visually impaired. Braille and Moon are composed of raised symbols that correspond to the letters of the alphabet. These raised symbols are used in combination to form words and sentences. Braille, based on raised dots, is a more complicated system to learn and is seen as too demanding for children who also have general learning disabilities (McLinden and Hendrickson 1996). The raised letters of the Moon system bear a resemblance to the letters of the alphabet as we know them.

Objects of reference

Objects of reference are specific objects that have a meaning assigned to them. They are often used with children who have multiple disabilities. Ockelford (1998: 3–4) gives the example of Peter, who is severely visually impaired and developmentally delayed.

> . . . the important thing [for Peter] was knowing when a given activity had finished . . . Peter was provided with a special tactile timetable, made up of a series of boxes in which different objects could be placed, each corresponding to a different activity. The boxes had lids that could be closed to indicate when something was over.

Tactile maps and virtual learning environments

Tactile maps can be produced to assist blind and visually impaired pupils in learning about the layout of their environment. Furthermore, computer technology allows individuals to explore and become familiar with locations through 'virtual environments'. The virtual environment can give pupils information about the size of a room, the size of objects and location of objects through either haptic (touch) feedback via a joystick or audio feedback of cane tapping, footstep sounds and echoes.

Hearing aids

Traditional hearing aids are basically amplifiers that pick up surrounding sounds and serve to make these sounds louder to the individual. **Cochlear implants** rely on sending electrical signals directly to the auditory nerve to provide a sensation of hearing.

Ways of developing communication and language with the hearing impaired

Auditory-oral approaches using hearing aids and implants aim to amplify residual hearing (i.e. make the best of what hearing ability exists) so that children can develop listening skills and spoken language.

Total communication is a view that sees hearing impaired children using different methods of communication. So in addition to using residual hearing, children would be encouraged to lip-read and use a sign system such as British Sign Language. British Sign Language is a visual language that uses hand shapes, facial expressions, gestures and body language to communicate.

Makaton is a simplified sign system that is used with individuals (both deaf and hearing) who have severe communication difficulties combined with learning disabilities.

Case study 4.13

Supporting a pupil with visual impairments

Simon wore glasses but still had difficulties seeing notes written on the whiteboard. Simon was in Year 6 at a mainstream junior school. The teacher ensured that all classroom work was presented to Simon on handouts. The teaching assistant, who was responsible for supporting Simon, would enlarge these handouts so that Simon could read them. Simon found reading material on a white background difficult as the glare interfered with his reading the words. It was suggested to the school that Simon should use coloured overlays to enhance the clarity of the text. As there were other pupils in the school who had difficulties with vision, the doors in every classroom were painted a different colour from the walls and the door handle was in a contrasting colour. This ensured that pupils could see the door and door handle and could easily enter and leave the classroom unaided.

Physical impairment

Physical impairment is a term that includes many conditions. Some of the more common conditions include muscular dystrophy, cystic fibrosis, spina bifida, cerebral palsy, diabetes and epilepsy.

The sort of challenges that might occur and how to deal with these challenges

As there are so many different types of physical impairment, this section on areas of difficulty and ways forward will focus on general concerns and strategies.

Movement

Many pupils with physical disabilities will have restricted movement. **Physiotherapists** and **occupational therapists** assess and help treat disorders of movement. Physiotherapists use exercise, manipulation and heat to help treat the condition, whereas an occupational therapist is interested in what daily living skills an individual has. Occupational therapists are also responsible for the assessment and provision of suitable equipment and for suggesting how to adapt the environment of home, school or work so the individual can be as independent as possible.

For example, a pupil with cerebral palsy might have difficulties with movement; they might be in a wheelchair and have stiffness in their muscles. Physiotherapists will advise parents and carers how best to lift and position an individual. In terms of the educational environment, they will advise on the best posture, working environment and seating for the child. If there is stiffness in the muscles, the physiotherapist will suggest certain exercises and physical activity that can help promote good patterns of movement. An occupational therapist would be involved in assessing what skills are missing and whether these physical and learning skills can be developed through the use of specialized equipment. Such equipment could include adapted tricycles or a gait trainer, designed to encourage walking.

Speech and language

The role of the speech and language therapist is to help individuals make the maximum use of their communication skills. A speech and language therapist will work with all individuals who have difficulties with their speech, understanding spoken and/or written language, using language, and eating and drinking. Some children will have delayed language due to limited opportunities to play and explore; the speech and language therapist, working with other therapists, can suggest suitable learning activities. Some physical conditions, such as cerebral palsy, will affect the motor movements responsible for talking, and in some cases an alternative system of communication might be suggested. For individuals who have good motor control in their hands and arms, a sign language might be appropriate. For others, a communication board where individuals point to letters, pictures or symbols might be more suitable.

Encouraging a sense of independence

Regardless of disability, everyone would like to be treated with respect and dignity. Many adults with physical disabilities will say that it is society's attitudes to them that are the most difficult to deal with. This attitude can be summed up by the expression 'Would they like sugar?' Children with physical disabilities need to be helped to be as independent as possible. All pupils need to be encouraged to make choices.

As a teaching assistant it is important to know and understand the needs of the particular pupil you are supporting. In many cases you will be putting into practice many of the interventions suggested by the various therapists.

Case study 4.14

Encouraging a sense of independence

Claire, age nine, attends a special school. She has cerebral palsy and no spoken communication. Owing to Claire's difficulty in controlling the movements of her arms, a sign language was not seen as appropriate.

However, Claire can point to objects. She can also shake her head to indicate yes or no, and she has a beautiful smile and laugh when she is happy. At school Claire loves the multi-sensory room. **Multi-sensory rooms** offer a range of experiences involving sight, sound, touch and smell. What Claire likes best is moving the specially adapted switches that control the combinations of light and sound. Claire's teacher believes that this helps Claire feel that she has control over her environment. When Claire started at the school, careful thought was given as to how the school could offer Claire meaningful choices. It was decided that when Claire was involved in any activity she would be given a choice between two activities. When she is involved in a literacy session she would be given a choice between listening to the story on tape or having someone read to her. When Claire is in the swimming pool, she is given a choice about what colour flotation device she holds on to. As the teacher said, 'It is through constantly having choices about all aspects of her life that we can best encourage a sense of independence.'

Bilingual and multilingual pupils

When working with bilingual and multilingual pupils, you need to know the language background of each child. Some children might come from a background where they have an understanding of two languages, e.g. they talk to mother in Spanish and talk to Dad in English. However, other children might come from a family that has recently immigrated or received refugee status and understand no, or very little, English. To recap what was said in Chapter 2, a child beginning school with no English will usually take two years to develop basic interpersonal communication skills and five to seven years to achieve cognitive academic language proficiency, the standard necessary to cope with GCSEs.

Hester (Barrs *et al.* 1988) outlined four stages of language development as: (1) new to English, (2) becoming familiar with English, (3) becoming confident as a user of English, and (4) a very fluent user of English in most social and learning contexts. Pupils who have already learned to read and write in their first language will show the following behaviours at the above stages of second language development (Hall 1995: 36).

Stage 1: New to English
- Pupil will listen and respond mainly in first language.
- Pupil is often silent in class; uses second language to say single words and simple phrases.
- Pupil can read simple words; relies on pictures for clues to meaning.
- Pupil begins to spell single words and begins to spell phonetically.

Stage 2: Becoming familiar with English
- Pupil will need to have all instructions repeated. However, the pupil can understand some of what is being said in class and can follow simple instructions and explanations.
- Pupil now participates in informal discussions and begins to participate in group work.
- Pupil begins to understand some of the material that is read and becomes able to discuss what has been read.
- Pupil can now write short passages; begins to use punctuation and begins to understand language rules such as present and future tense.

Stage 3: Becoming confident as a language user
- Pupil now understands a great deal of what is being said and can follow complex instructions.
- Pupil becomes more confident in speaking. At this point spoken language still exceeds reading and spelling ability.
- Pupil is able to read and understand more complex texts.
- Writing skills have improved but pupil will still make mistakes in regard to difficult vocabulary and complex grammatical constructions.

Stage 4: Fluent
- Pupil is now fluent in regard to listening and speaking in the second language.
- Pupil is a capable and confident reader and can now skim read.
- Pupil can confidently write in a number of different styles.

The sort of challenges that might occur and possible explanations for such challenges

The child is exceptionally quiet in class

This could be part of the normal stage of second language acquisition. However, if a child starts school and is delayed in their first language, then an assessment of their first language abilities needs to be carried out to determine the extent of the delay. This is necessary to establish whether there are any additional special needs.

The child is not progressing

Hall (1995) gives a number of possible reasons for a child not progressing. Firstly, the work set might be too difficult. A teacher might wrongly assume on the basis of the pupil's confidence in informal conversations that they understand more than they do. An ability to communicate on an informal level does not necessarily mean that the pupil will understand abstract academic language.

It is not surprising that bilingual and multilingual students can suffer from environmental stress, maybe as a result of bullying and racism. If the child is from a refugee family there could also be, depending on family circumstances, financial stress and painful emotional memories stemming from their life in their country of origin. All of these stresses can impact on their academic progress.

If neither of these explanations seems to fit, then an assessment for special needs, such as dyslexia, needs to be carried out.

How to deal with these challenges

There are a number of suggestions:

- In the early stages of language development it is suggested that the first language be used within the classroom to support learning. It is recommended that a bilingual assistant support the child for at least some of the time.
- If there is a group of pupils who share the same first language, it is felt that it would not be a good idea to put them all in one group. It would be better to have mixed groups of children, i.e. a few children who are beginning to learn English with the majority of children who are fluent in English. In this case the fluent speakers can help and serve as role models for the children who are beginning to learn English.
- It is important for children who are trying to learn a second language to be seated with pupils who will support and help them.
- Use bilingual or translated texts.
- The work set will need to be differentiated. Differentiation has been defined as adapting work to the differing capabilities of pupils with the aim of supporting learning. The work needs to be geared to their understanding but at the same time be suitably age-appropriate, motivating, and cognitively and intellectually demanding.

Thinking deeply

Sarah was working as an HLTA at a large secondary school which served a predominantly white working-class catchment area. In recent years, a large influx of pupils from Eastern Europe had enrolled in the school. There was a certain amount of tension within the school. Some of the Eastern European pupils complained that they felt lonely and consequently tended to stick together as a group. The Eastern European pupils felt that the English pupils were angry at them. Many of the Eastern European pupils had received comments telling them to go home and that their parents were stealing English jobs.

As a teaching assistant working in this school, how could you encourage inclusive interactions?

Looked after children

Looked after children are children in the care of the local authority. These children may be living in children's homes or, more likely, in foster care. There are a number of different types of foster care including short and long term, emergency, therapeutic, remand and kinship. What looked after children have in common is that they have been separated from their birth parents, that this separation involves trauma and that they are likely to underachieve at school. Statistics in England stated that as of 31 March 2009, there were 60,900 children in care and that 61 per cent of these children first came to the attention of social services due to abuse or neglect (DCSF 2009). In 2009, one-third of looked after children obtained no GCSEs and a further fifth obtained fewer than five GCSEs (The Poverty Site 2009). Reasons for low achievement are complex and include adverse experiences in infancy, family background, low expectations, multiple foster placements and multiple school moves. These statistics need to be seen in relation to the *Every Child Matters* goals of achievement and enjoyment. These statistics are alarming in that underachievement at school can lead to continuing disadvantage and exclusion in adult life. However, in stating these alarming statistics, it is also important to recognize individual differences and that some children rise to the challenges that life throws at them and go on to lead happy and successful adult lives.

The sort of challenges that might occur and possible explanations for such challenges

How a looked after child copes in the classroom depends very much on the individual child and the circumstances surrounding them. Some looked after children may exhibit challenging behaviour, they may have poor self-esteem and be prone to anxiety and depression. Again depending on circumstances and experiences, the child may be diagnosed with an attachment disorder or post-traumatic stress disorder. When working with a child who is looked after, it is very important to learn about their background. Sometimes it is only one child who is removed from the family and placed in care, so possibly a looked after child may have brothers and sisters who are still at home with the parents. It may also be the case that the looked after child has brothers or sisters who have been placed in other foster homes.

How to deal with these challenges

Be aware of potential flashpoints

Find out when family contact times are. Most children who are looked after will need support in managing their feelings coming up to a family visit and coping with their feelings after a visit. Again this will apply to any court cases or legal proceedings.

Avoid negative assumptions

Although the statistics for looked after children are alarming, these statistics could create a **self-fulfilling prophecy** if teaching staff believe that looked after children are not interested in school, not academically able and are likely to be troublemakers. It is important that those who work with looked after children have the same expectations for them as they do for all the other children in their classroom.

Handle sensitively

Pupils who are looked after need to be listened to but not singled out as being different from the other pupils. Teaching staff need to understand that the quality of their work may fluctuate if there are changes in their care arrangements. As with all other pupils, they need to be praised.

In addition, it is also important for teaching staff to know if a family fosters, because having a foster child in a family will have an impact on the birth children.

Gifted and talented pupils

Gifted and talented pupils are on the government's agenda as there is concern that schools are failing to identify their most able pupils and that these pupils are not sufficiently challenged or helped to reach their potential (Morris 2002). Gifted and talented pupils benefit from both extension activities, which go further, and enrichment activities, which go deeper. There are numerous definitions for gifted and talented, but to start this discussion we will look at Morgan's (2007) definitions: **gifted pupils** are those who achieve highly, i.e. in the top 5 per cent in one or more academic subjects, and **talented pupils** achieve highly in more practical and creative subjects such as sport, music and visual arts. However, in being inclusive, the government recommends that identification of gifted and talented pupils will reveal those with potential as well as those who are already achieving at a high level (DfCSF 2008: 10) and that this approach will allow pupils from all backgrounds to have an opportunity to express their ability in a range of different ways.

But how easy is it to identify who is gifted and talented?

Thinking deeply

Who is the gifted pupil and why?
Is it:

a a very hard working and motivated pupil who always gets straight As and always behaves well in class? or

b a pupil who is disruptive, clowns around in class and does not perform well?

Or could both a) and b) be gifted pupils?

The sort of challenges that might occur and possible explanations for such challenges

Adjustment difficulties

The research on whether gifted and talented pupils have difficulties in relating socially and emotionally to their peer group has been mixed. On one hand, some research has noted the potential difficulties gifted and talented pupils face in finding someone of their own age who is at the same level and has the same interests. This could lead to the pupil feeling isolated. Other research has pointed out that an early ability to intellectually understand abstract issues without underlying emotional understanding can lead to confusion and anxiety. However, further research has revealed that gifted children are at least as well adjusted as other children (Morgan 2007). So some pupils will have difficulties in relating to their peers, and others won't.

Consequences of labelling

The rationale for identifying pupils as gifted or talented is that they are then able to be appropriately challenged and supported in their learning. However, there are a number of consequences of having pupils know that they are on a gifted and talented register. It is possible that a hard-working pupil who is not labelled as gifted or talented may become de-motivated, whereas some pupils who are given such a label may be embarrassed or see it as an unwelcome pressure to achieve more. It is possible also that pupils who are removed from class for special input sessions may feel different from their peers and this could lead to difficulties in social relationships. And it is possible that when their names are entered on the register, some pupils might stop putting any effort into their schoolwork because they feel that as they are so bright they don't need to work – many teachers tell stories of the extremely bright and gifted pupils who fail to live up to their potential. What this highlights is the relationship between potential and actual

Table 4.3 A comparison between the mystery and mastery models of giftedness

Belief	Mystery model	Mastery model
What is the theory that explains the nature of giftedness and talent?	Some people are born gifted and/or talented and others are not. Once gifted, always gifted.	Being talented and/ or gifted develops over time as a result of appropriate opportunities to learn.
What is the relationship between effort and being gifted and/or talented?	Those pupils who are gifted or talented do not need to work – their abilities come easily without them having to try.	All achievements require hard work, sustained effort and persistence in the face of difficulties.
Are there differences in how long it takes to learn?	Gifted pupils learn very quickly.	All learning requires time and is often slow.

Source: adapted from Matthews and Folsom (2009)

achievement and the relationship between ability and effort. (For further information on the relationship between ability and effort, see pages 187–8.) Many theorists now make a distinction between a mystery model and a mastery model of giftedness.

The mystery and mastery models have been equated with fixed and growth mindsets, which will be discussed further on pages 187–8. But what is important with the mastery model is that being gifted and/or talented is now seen as a process and that effort cannot be separated from ability. Many educators talk of creating learning opportunities that can lead to gifted-level learning. Now the emphasis is how pupils learn to act in ways that leads others (teachers and parents) to see them as gifted. A definition of giftedness that fits into the mastery model is 'an exceptionally advanced subject-specific ability at a particular point in time such that a pupil's learning needs cannot be well met without significant adaptations to the curriculum' (Matthews and Foster 2005: 26).

How to deal with these challenges

If the pupils are experiencing difficulties with their peers then they will need support. (For further information on friendships, see pages 37–40.)

Those involved in supporting teaching and learning need to focus on the relationship between ability and effort – that trying hard makes you more able. (For further information on the relationship between ability and effort, see pages 187–8.)

And remember, all pupils, not just the gifted and talented, need to develop thinking skills.

Thinking deeply

Anwar was on the school's gifted and talented register. Anwar had a real flair for maths, and in maths class he was given special extension activities. When his previous worksheet was given back, Anwar was mortified when he realized that he had got two questions wrong – Anwar never got maths questions wrong.

Anwar asked the teaching assistant: 'Now that I have got two questions wrong, does that mean I am no longer gifted and talented?'

How would you answer Anwar?

Pupils with poor working memory

Simply put, working memory is a mental notepad for storing necessary information for everyday activities. Working memory makes connections between new incoming information and information that is held in long-term memory. In a classroom situation, a pupil will use working memory to follow directions and instructions and keep track of progress. Working memory involves the processing of verbal and visual-spatial information, and has a component that allocates attention.

Let us see how working memory works with an example. A pupil hears the teacher saying, 'Do you remember yesterday's session on fractions and the diagram we had on the board?' The pupil listening to this retrieves the relevant information from his memory and possibly is able to visualize in his mind's eye the diagram the teacher had on the board the day before. The teacher then asks the pupils to open their textbooks and go to page 5, look at diagram 3b and answer questions 4 through to 7. Some pupils can easily do this task, but pupils with low or poor working memory will find the teacher's request extremely difficult.

Working memory is essential for moment-to-moment interaction. However, information in working memory is easily lost through distraction and memory overload. Individuals differ on working memory ability; i.e. the amount of information they are able to retain and process in their mind at any one point in time. It is estimated that approximately 10 per cent of children have poor working memory (Gathercole and Alloway 2008). The good news is that low or poor working memory can be identified by IQ tests (see pages 102–5) and screening tests.

The sort of challenges that might occur

Gathercole and Alloway (2008) have identified that pupils with poor working memory will:

* often make slow progress in academic areas of learning such as reading and maths
* appear to have short attention spans and be easily distracted
* have difficulty following instructions, they may forget where they are on a task, skip important steps or abandon the task altogether, and
* have difficulty doing two things at once.

How to deal with these challenges

As a teaching assistant who works closely with the pupils, it is important that you recognize and mention to the teacher any pupils whom you suspect have difficulties in working memory. Screening tools can be useful in identifying how much pupils can remember at any one point in time.

Working memory loads can be reduced by keeping instructions and tasks simple and within the pupils' working memory ability or capacity. You should repeat important information.

The good news is that working memory capacity or abilities can be developed by teaching pupils memory aids and specific strategies such as rehearsal and elaboration. An example of the strategy of elaboration would be to have children create stories of the objects or items they need to remember.

Putting it all together

In the beginning of this chapter it was stated that every child is unique and has their own profile of gifts, strengths and weaknesses. This is true for all

Figure 11 James's idea of working memory was not quite the same as his teacher's.

your pupils, including those with additional needs. Using the knowledge incorporated in this chapter, consider case study 4.15.

Case study 4.15

A pupil with multiple special needs

Mary works in a mainstream school supporting the Year 6 class. One of the pupils Mary supports is Alison. Alison has both Asperger's syndrome and dyslexia, and she is extremely gifted at drawing. Mary recalls a recent lesson:

> The teacher had assigned the class an essay to write and I was sitting with Alison working through an essay plan. I told Alison that once she had finished her story she could then draw a picture. If Alison had her way, she would do nothing but drawing.
>
> In terms of writing Alison also prefers to write her rough work in pencil. However, her pencils always have to be sharpened up to a certain level for her to write. When Alison is somewhat anxious about work she tends to press too hard on her pencil, which means she has to get up and go to the back of the class to get her favourite sharpener. I have suggested that we have the sharpener on her desk but Alison is firm that the pencil sharpener is kept at the back of the class. Well, off Alison went to get the sharpener, but on her way back to her seat I noticed that Alison hit every pupil she passed with the pencil sharpener. The pencil sharpener was very light and most pupils just smiled and said: 'Oh, it's you, Alison', but I could tell that a few of the pupils were fed up. Anyway, it was then time to go out for break, but I noticed that Alison was all by herself – and not for the first time that week.

Thinking deeply

What challenges does Alison face?
   How would you support Alison?

Chapter 5

Managing behaviour for learning

Introduction

It has been widely recognized that managing classroom behaviour is necessary for effective teaching to occur. This chapter will look at ways of dealing with inappropriate behaviour as well as highlighting the need to be proactive and focus on the behaviours that pupils need in order to learn. Prior to the 1970s, approaches to behaviour management emphasized how best to respond to episodes of challenging behaviour, while after the 1970s, the advice was to take a proactive approach that focused on classroom organization and creating positive relationships with pupils (Jones and Jones 1995). Interestingly, research on what makes for effective teachers revealed teachers who were very good at preventing inappropriate behaviour (Good and Brophy 1987). As a result of these findings, advice regarding behaviour management now focuses on creating positive classroom environments, building positive relationships with pupils, teaching pupils skills to enable them to self-manage their own behaviour, and dealing effectively with conflicts and crisis situations (Meadows and Melloy 1996).

Nowadays we talk about positive behaviour management and behaviour for learning. However, it is clear that while the emphasis should be on the positive, inappropriate behaviour continues to be an issue.

Despite moral panics in the media describing classrooms in chaos and 'feral children' running amok, a recent Ofsted (2005a) report found that 90 per cent of behaviour in primary schools and 68 per cent in secondary schools was either excellent or good. In contrast, unsatisfactory behaviour was found in only 1 per cent of primary schools and 9 per cent of secondary schools. This report (Ofsted 2005a: 5), while recognizing that the majority of pupils work hard and behave well, noted that in even the most well-managed schools, pockets of low-level disruptive behaviour such as constant chatter, talking out of turn and episodes of inattention can have a negative impact on staff and pupil learning and create an atmosphere where more serious incidents are likely to occur.

In highlighting the range of behaviour that those involved with supporting teaching and learning may experience, Daniels *et al.* (1999: 145–6, 164) describe how unacceptable and problematic behaviour can be classified according to severity, with level 1 being the least problematic and level 3 being behaviour of a very serious nature.

While these levels are not definitive in that they do not outline every possible example of inappropriate or challenging behaviour, they do illustrate the range of challenges those involved in supporting teaching and learning could face.

Table 5.1 Classifying problematic behaviours

Level 1

- Disrupting other children. Chatting in class. Not on task. Out of seat. Wandering about the class. Fidgeting in seat.
- Forgets to bring in needed equipment or materials. Arrives late. Careless damage to property.
- Answers back. Makes inappropriate noises. Minor bad language.
- Difficulty in getting on with other pupils in the class. Difficulty in sharing and cooperating with others. Tells lies with the intention of getting others in trouble. Sometimes emotional. Minor problems in self-esteem.

Level 2

- More of level 1 behaviour.
- Deliberate defiance. Refusal to do work or follow instructions.
- Threatening behaviour to other pupils and teachers. Incidents of bullying. Isolated acts of violence, e.g. hitting, kicking, punching, etc.
- Easily reduced to tears. Easily reduced to outbursts of anger and tantrums. Withdrawn. Isolated from peer group. Problems with self-esteem. Cannot express feelings.
- Minor vandalism and stealing.

Level 3

- More of level 2 behaviour.
- Persistent episodes of defiance, abusive language and bullying.
- Creates major disruptions in class on a regular basis.
- Frequent episodes of aggressive behaviour causing deliberate injury.
- Serious acts of vandalism to school buildings and property.
- Often leaves school premises without consent.

Source: after Daniels *et al.* (1999)

In 2006 Ofsted recommended simple strategies in positive behaviour management, including ensuring that all staff know what behaviours are to be considered acceptable or unacceptable and that they know what to do when faced with such behaviour.

A school will have policies in place in regard to managing behaviour. Therefore, when inappropriate behaviour occurs, whether it be low-level disruption or incidences of very challenging behaviour, all those involved in supporting teaching and learning should know what is required of them.

Thinking deeply

What is your role and responsibilities in the event of pupils:

- chatting in class?
- not being on task?
- being out of their seats?
- wandering about the classroom?
- fidgeting in their seats?
- persistently being defiant?
- using abusive language?
- bullying?

How do you strike a balance between focusing on the positive and administering sanctions?

In supporting teaching and learning, it is important to note that some children and young people will be identified as having behavioural, emotional and social difficulties (BESD). The DfES's *Code of Practice* (2001: 87) describes these pupils as:

> . . . withdrawn or isolated, disruptive and disturbing, hyperactive and lack concentration; those with immature social skills; and those presenting challenging behaviours arising from other complex special needs.'

The difficulties pupils with BESD face may create a barrier to learning and they may need special educational provision. It is also possible that a pupil may have an underlying learning disability that may intensify behaviour and emotional difficulties (DfES 2001: 87).

In these circumstances, those involved in supporting teaching and learning need to seek advice from teachers and SENCOs regarding appropriate strategies.

Aspects of culture, upbringing, home circumstances and physical and emotional health that could influence the pupil's interactions with others

There are many outside influences that could explain or account for a pupil's behaviour. Possibly the pupil has learned to behave in such a disruptive way. The behaviourists (see Chapter 1) state that there is always a reason for any behaviour. This viewpoint would argue that if a pupil continually behaves in a challenging or disturbing manner then it is because they have in the past been rewarded for this type of behaviour. Attention can be a reward. Any attention, even negative attention such as a teacher screaming and yelling at them, is better than no attention. Pupils might get attention and respect from their peers for acting up. Being thrown out of a class might be preferable to being in a class where they have no idea of how to do the work; moreover, acting up and being sent out prevents other pupils from finding out that they can't actually do the work. If a pupil can't succeed academically, perhaps they can succeed at being a failure.

Bandura (see Chapter 1), in his social learning theory, would argue that pupils learn disruptive and challenging behaviour by observing and imitating others. Pupils can learn inappropriate behaviour by watching what happens to other pupils who behave in such a way at school. Pupils might observe and learn disruptive behaviour in their home environment, in the playground or out in the streets with their friends.

Harris (1997), in outlining her **group socialization theory**, argues that it is the group that an individual belongs to that determines their behaviour. For a pupil this group would be their peer group. A pupil would learn rules about what is appropriate behaviour from the peer group. A problem often occurs when the peer group, culture or subculture that the pupil identifies with is in conflict with the culture of the school. For example, the culture of the school would promote values and attitudes such as respect for other pupils and staff, commitment to learning, pursuit of academic, social and athletic excellence, wearing the school uniform with pride, etc. However, not all peer groups and subcultures would see these attitudes as desirable and there lies the problem. For some pupils, handing in homework, being seen to work in class and doing what they are told would not be seen as being 'cool'.

Another aspect that influences the pupil's interactions with others is *mental health*. Although professionals in the health and social care fields will use terms such as mental health and mental health difficulties; professionals in education will often use terms such as emotional health and well-being.

(For further information on aspects of emotional health, see pages 41–4.) The DfEE (2001: iv) defines mental health as:

... maintaining a good level of personal and social functioning. For children and young people, this means getting on with others, both peers and adults, participating in educative and other social activities and having a positive self-esteem. Mental health is about coping and adjusting to the demands of growing up.

While this definition stresses what children should be working towards, the DfEE (2001:1) says problems with mental health in children and young adults could include:

- Eating disorders: anorexia nervosa, bulimia nervosa.
- Emotional disorders: excessive fears, anxiety, depression.
- Conduct disorders: stealing, setting fires, torturing animals, aggression.
- Attachment disorders: 'Children who are markedly distressed or socially impaired as a result of an extremely abnormal pattern of attachment to parents or major care-givers.'

Emotional health continues to be an important issue; Emmerson and Hatton (2007) describe how over one in three children and adolescents with a learning disability in Britain have a diagnosable psychiatric disorder. In discussing mental health issues, much research has gone into identifying risk and resilience factors. **Risk factors** suggest that there are situations that can make a child more susceptible or more likely to have mental health problems, whereas **resilience factors** serve to protect the child from mental health problems.

Risk factors include:

- Child has or has had insecure relationships with parents or caregivers, has low self-esteem, specific learning disabilities, experienced academic failure.
- Family is characterized by hostile relationships and open conflict. The family unit has experienced breakdown and is unable to provide clear and consistent discipline. The family unit might be coping with issues such as death, bereavement, mental illness in a family member or a family member in prison. In severe cases, the child might experience physical, emotional or sexual abuse within the family. In general, the family is unable to meet the needs of the child.

- The environment in which the child lives is disadvantaged. There is a high level of poverty, homelessness and limited social opportunities.

Resilience factors include:

- Child has or has had secure relationships with parents or caregivers, is average or above average level of intelligence, has good social and communication skills, is willing to seek and accept help and advice, and has a sense of humour and a religious faith.
- At least one parent provides affection, love, emotional support and clear and consistent discipline, and encourages the child in educational achievement.
- The environment in which the child lives has many advantages. There are good housing, high employment rates, a high standard of living, good community relationships and many affordable social opportunities. (DfEE 2001: 4–6)

Furthermore, there is much that a school community can do to develop resiliency: supportive caring relationships can transform pupils' lives; consistent high expectations can provide structure, security and safety; and opportunities for meaningful participation can bolster a sense of belonging and self-worth. Staff attitudes towards pupils can also make a difference, with staff being recommended to focus on pupil strengths rather than deficits. An Ofsted report (2005b: 2) entitled 'Healthy Minds' found that schools that were best at promoting emotional health and well-being respected and valued every individual and had very good systems to deal with pupil difficulties and bullying.

Thinking deeply

What do you think resilience means?

Do you believe resilience means 'taking it on the chin', i.e. accepting what life has to offer and getting on with it?

Do you believe that resilience is genetic, i.e. either an individual is born with this trait or they are not?

Or do you believe that resilience is something that can be developed, and if so, how?

Thinking deeply

Wolin (2004) states that schools can make a difference and that those involved in supporting teaching and learning have the ability to transform children and young people's lives through small everyday gestures, what Masten (2001) refers to as 'ordinary magic'.

What ordinary magic do you perform on a daily basis?

Intervention strategies

As challenging and problematic behaviour exists on many levels, so do intervention strategies. Most teaching assistants will be directly involved at the lower levels of intervention. Table 5.2 outlines strategies that teaching assistants might use. The examples show what teaching assistants can do daily to help the teacher create an environment where it is possible for all pupils to learn.

Thinking deeply

Many schools will have behaviour charters or posters displayed throughout the school. These posters come in all shapes, colours and sizes.

Do you have posters displayed in your classroom?

What does the poster tell the pupils to do? Does it tell the pupil how to behave? Does it tell the pupils how to study?

Who creates these posters?

How do you use these posters? Are they just wallpaper?

Do you refer to the poster when talking to pupils about issues regarding behaviour?

What does the poster communicate about the values of your school?

Does the poster help make positive behaviour happen?

Despite all the positive interventions, there will be times when situations arise of a more serious nature and the role of a teaching assistant is to inform a teacher of what is happening. Schools will have codes of behaviour and established ways of dealing with very disruptive behaviour. Schools will use sanctions such as detentions, loss of privileges, or requiring pupils to stay in at break. At a secondary level, the school might operate an 'on-call system', where if a teacher is in difficulty, they ask a cooperative pupil to take a card to the office. This will signal that the teacher needs assistance. A senior member of staff will then come to the class and remove the disruptive pupil from the class. In the event of very serious episodes of challenging

Table 5.2 Intervention strategies a teaching assistant might use

Intervention strategies	Example of teaching assistant intervention
Reminding of rules and codes of behaviour. This can be given to groups or on an individual basis. It can be given before an activity or during an activity to remind the group how they should be behaving.	The following strategy is used with a reception class. 'Now, Orange Group, before we start we need to remind ourselves of our listening rules. In order to listen we need to put on our thinking heads.' (Teaching assistant points to head.) 'We need to listen with our ears.' (Points to ears.) 'We need to listen with our eyes.' (Points to eyes.) 'We need to listen with our mouth.' (Points to mouth.) 'And we need to listen with our hands.' (Holds out hands.) 'Shall we repeat that? Now if anyone forgets, I will point to the rule on the board.'
Giving 'the look'.	When I am supporting the teacher during the literacy hour, I sit at the front facing the children. If I see one of the children doing something they shouldn't be, I try to get their attention and then I give them a look and mouth 'Behave!' This often works.
Moving closer to pupils. Separating disruptive pupils.	I work in a secondary school. When I am in class, and I realize there is a disturbance in some part of the room, I will go over to the pupils and casually ask how things are going. Sometimes this is enough to get them back on task. When I work with groups, sometimes there are two pupils who just cannot get on or sometimes they are getting on too well and they are not doing their work. If that is the case, I get the pupils to change places. If this doesn't work and one pupil is disrupting the others and preventing them from working, I ask the teacher if I can move the disruptive pupil to somewhere quieter.

Intervention strategies	Example of teaching assistant intervention
Chatting privately with the pupil.	I work in a secondary school. My job is to support several pupils who have statements; that is, a statement of special educational needs. One day Jason was getting very wound up by another pupil. It was not that this pupil was saying anything to Jason but I knew that Jason and the other pupil did not get on. I asked the teacher if I could have a quiet chat with Jason in the hall for a few minutes. I reminded Jason of his behaviour targets and how well he had been doing and I asked him if he could remember what he felt bothered by another pupil. He said that he should try to ignore it. After that we went back in the class and Jason worked very well. I felt I needed to take him outside as what I wanted to say to him was better said in confidence.
Giving choices and warning of consequences.	Whenever a pupil is misbehaving, I will remind them of what they should be doing. If they don't do what they should be doing, I give them another chance. I say to them, 'You have a choice. You can do what I say and get on with your work or I will have to inform the teacher of your behaviour.' If they still don't do what they should, then I inform the teacher. It is important that pupils know there are consequences for their actions.
Removing the audience.	I work in a junior school. I was working with a group working on a sheet on fractions. John told the group in a loud voice that he wasn't going to work and that he was going to go on strike and that school was useless. I moved John to a separate table. I removed the audience as I felt that most of what he said was said to impress the others. I asked him, 'What is the matter?' At first he didn't say anything, but then he finally admitted he had forgotten how to do fractions.

(continued)

Table 5.2 (continued)

Intervention strategies	Example of teaching assistant intervention
Using humour and boosting self-esteem.	Amy was very disappointed by her drawing of an elephant. She said she was going to rip it up. I then quickly got a piece of paper and drew an elephant. I said to her, 'Well, just look at my attempt. It looks more like my Aunt Ethel.' Amy laughed and felt much better about her picture.
Encouraging empathy and respect.	Whenever a pupil swears at me, I ask them if I ever swear at them. They say no. I then ask how they like it when someone swears at them. I then say, 'Well I expect you to treat me with the same respect that I treat you.'
Asking pupil to behave in a manner that expects the pupil to respond.	For example, 'Joe, we have a rule about sharing play equipment at break. I expect you to give others a turn on the bike. Thank you.'
Using positive strategies such as rewarding appropriate good behaviour, praise, stickers, merit points.	Jason has a history of winding other pupils up and starting fights. After he had worked quietly all lesson and completed his worksheet, I said how good his work was and how proud I was of his behaviour.

behaviour, the parents of the pupil will be brought in and, in some cases, pupils will be excluded from the school. If a pupil is having difficulties of an emotional nature, e.g. with depression or anxiety, the school will refer the pupil to counsellors or pastoral support.

The importance of recognizing and rewarding positive behaviour

We have talked previously about the many reasons why a pupil displays disruptive behaviour. Although reprimands are used on pupils, the most effective way of dealing with disruptive behaviour is to reward appropriate and good behaviour, i.e. 'Catch them while they are being good.' If you notice a child doing something good, tell them immediately. Many educators will say that verbal reinforcement is one of the most fundamental tools available to those supporting teaching and learning, and that it is both powerful and meaningful for pupils. However, in order for the rewards to be effective, the pupil must know what behaviour they are being rewarded for. Rewards motivate the pupil to repeat the good behaviour and serve to boost the pupil's self-esteem.

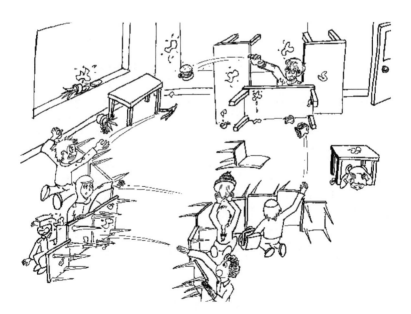

Figure 12 Although behaviour can be challenging, teaching assistants need to model appropriate behaviour.

Case study 5.1

Taking the 'catching them while they are being good' challenge

Joanna worked as a teaching assistant in a busy junior school and was convinced that she used this strategy on a daily basis. Having agreed to the challenge, Joanna asked the HLTA in the school to come into her classroom and observe her for an hour using the tally sheet listed in Table 5.3. Joanna was shocked at how few times she actually praised pupils for their good behaviour. As Joanna stated: 'It is funny that what I thought I did was not actually what I did do.'

Thinking deeply

Are you willing to take the 'catching them while they are being good' challenge?

The Trouble with Gold Stars

Kohn (2000) sounds a cautionary note in his book *Punished by Rewards: The Trouble with Gold Stars, Incentive Plans, A's, Praise and Other Bribes*, arguing that rewards and sanctions produce pupils who will temporarily do what is expected of them but that this prevents them from becoming responsible decision makers. In a sense, this view looks at the motivation behind behaviour. Is a pupil behaving or completing a task just to earn a gold star or a merit, or are they engaging in the task because they personally see the value of the task or behaviour? As educators, when we praise pupils for their good behaviour we are hoping that in time they will internalize concepts of what is good and fair and that their internal sense of right and wrong will guide them in future behaviour. (For further information on moral development, see pages 44–7, and on intrinsic motivation, see pages 186–7.)

Developing thinking skills: giving choices and stating consequences

Pupils need to be helped to see that they are in part responsible for what happens to them.

Table 5.3 Catching them while they are being good!

Behaviours praised by teaching assistant	Number of times observed
Coming into the classroom quickly and quietly	
Working hard on a piece of work	
Putting their hand up and waiting to be asked	
Providing a good idea or suggestion in a discussion	
Taking turns; waiting for their turn	
Bringing appropriate books and equipment to the lesson	
Being willing to try something new or difficult	
Sharing equipment	
Starting work quickly	
Other examples: (please specify)	

Source: adapted from Cousins and Jennings (2003)

Case study 5.2

Daniel learns to be responsible for his behaviour and its consequences

Daniel:	Mr Todd gave me a detention.
Sara (TA):	What did you do?
Daniel:	I didn't do anything. Mr Todd is always picking on me.
Sara (TA):	Tell me exactly what happened.
Daniel:	Mr Todd said I was bullying Ted. I wasn't bullying. I did have my arm round his neck but I was just mucking about.

Of course at this point Sara, the teaching assistant, is not surprised that Daniel got a detention. However, Daniel might not have been aware of how his behaviour was affecting others. Pupils need to be told how their behaviour makes other people feel. Moreover, in order to improve the pupil's behaviour, the pupil first needs to be aware of why he or she received a detention. Pupils need to be aware that they have choices in how they behave and that every choice has a consequence. Pupils need to be aware that they can make good choices or bad choices.

Case study 5.2 (continued)

Sara (TA):   If you put your arm round someone else's neck, they might think that you are trying to strangle them. If a teacher sees you doing it, they will think the same and you will be accused of bullying. If you bully someone then the consequence is that you will be in trouble and that you will have a detention. If you mind your own business and get on with work, then you won't get a detention. The choice is up to you.

This strategy can be used to both reflect on why a pupil got into trouble and as a means of preventing future incidents.

Thinking deeply

Imagine that you are supporting a pupil, Malcolm, who has difficulties with anger management. From observing how Malcolm behaves, you quickly realize that other pupils seem to know just what to say to wind him up and that Malcolm always seems to fall for it. This is particularly relevant when Malcolm is on the football pitch. Opponents will deliberately say things to Malcolm to get him riled and this always seems to end in Malcolm punching someone and being sent off.

How would you get Malcolm to realize for himself that he has choices in how to respond?

Being proactive: monitoring the group to spot signs of conflict at an early stage

It is obviously better to prevent a major incident than to have to deal with it. But to prevent an incident, you need to be sensitive to the cues, both verbal and non-verbal, that indicate that a pupil is 'building up to' an episode of challenging behaviour. However, different pupils will react differently, and so observation and knowledge of the pupils you are working with are crucial.

Hewett (2000) listed the following non-verbal signs to look out for in your 'at risk' pupil:

- Becomes restless, gets out of their seat and paces the classroom, or becomes very still and quiet.
- Increases eye contact or becomes reluctant to make eye contact; eyes widen.

- Shows facial tension; makes threatening gestures, e.g. clenched fists; trembles all over; is attempting self-control, e.g. clasping hands; face is going red or white.
- Invades personal space, e.g. 'in your face'.
- Demonstrates inconsistent and unusual behaviour.

Hewett (2000) says there are also verbal signs to look out for:

- Mutters phrases (e.g. 'No one ever f ****** listens. You're all the same.'). Makes threats (e.g. 'I'm going to get you!').
- Performs in front of an audience, trying to get audience on their side.
- Voice becomes louder and higher in pitch. Inappropriate laughter.

De-escalation strategies

Hewett (2000) suggests a number of ways to make a potentially dangerous situation less dangerous:

- If there are others pupils in the room and they are in potential danger, then they should be removed. This also removes the audience, which may help defuse the situation.
- If you know what has triggered the outburst, sometimes removing the trigger can defuse the situation.
- Allow space between you and the aggressor. If possible, make sure the pupil has an escape route. In extreme cases, think about how you would get out of the situation and consider which pieces of school equipment could be used as a weapon against you.
- Keep normal eye contact. Try to appear calm and non-confrontational. Do not stand too close. Do not stand 'square-on', but rather at an angle. Don't make matters worse by losing your temper. Talk softly. Try to get the pupil to calm down. Wait for assistance.
- Sometimes it is helpful to try to distract the pupil by focusing them on something completely different.
- Sometimes all you can do is stand back, do nothing and wait until the person has calmed down.

Recovery strategies

Let's take, for example, a situation where a Year 9 pupil blows up in class, throws several chairs around and in the process breaks a window. Once it seems the worst is over and the pupil is calming down, the pupil is said to be in the recovery phase. At this point, teaching staff need to avoid doing things that could make the pupil engage in further acts of aggression. No matter what the pupil has done, what they need at this stage is reassurance and compassion. Avoid blaming the pupil and act positively towards them. At some point, the pupil will need to talk about their behaviour; however, pupils will differ in terms of when they will be ready to talk. Of course it is difficult to be calm and reassuring to someone who has acted in a totally inappropriate manner. Counsellors often talk about how you can condemn the behaviour but still value the person (Hewett 2000).

Thinking deeply

Behaviour for learning – what is this all about?
  What range of behaviours do pupils need to develop in order to learn?
  How can you support pupils in developing these skills?

Chapter 6

Establishing effective working relationships with pupils and colleagues

Basic principles of effective communication with pupils

The role of teaching assistants is to work with the teacher in order to support the learning of pupils. To support learning, a teaching assistant must communicate effectively with pupils. Effective communication is said to happen when there is open and honest communication, when dialogue is handled in a constructive manner, and when there is consistent and effective support. These are the principles of effective communication. But maybe a little more needs to be said about what these principles actually mean in practice.

- *Open and honest communication.* The pupil should feel able to say what they are truly feeling. However, this requires that the pupil trusts the teaching assistant. In turn the teaching assistant should be open and honest with the pupil. This sounds great, but how do you say those things that are difficult to say, e.g. 'If you weren't so bone idle, I am sure you could do your work', and, on the other hand, how do you respond when a pupil says 'I hate you'? This brings us on to the second principle.
- *Ability to handle dialogue in a constructive manner.* So it seems that although we should aim for open and honest communication, the way we talk to or respond to a pupil should be conducted in a manner that is positive, sensitive to the feelings of others and that does not undermine a pupil's self-esteem. Again it is important to use constructive feedback. (For more information on constructive feedback, see page 71.) Communication that follows these principles will serve as an example to the pupils of how adults should talk to each other.

- *Consistent and effective support.* This principle states that constructive and honest communication needs to be consistent, i.e. we should try to act in this way to all pupils at all times.

The next sections on active listening and interpreting body language give suggestions and handy tips on how we can effectively communicate with pupils.

Thinking deeply

Can you recall a situation when you really felt that you were listened to?
What was it that made you feel this way?
Can you recall a situation when you felt that you were not listened to?
What was it that made you feel this way?
How do you listen to pupils?

Techniques of active listening

As individuals we have conversations all the time and listening to what others say is an important part of a conversation. However, there is a difference between **active listening** and social listening, which we do on an everyday basis. Active listening involves communicating, or showing to the person we are talking to, that we have heard what they have said and that we understand what they are saying. Sometimes this type of listening is referred to as 'rewarding listening'. The following outlines a ten-skill approach to 'rewarding listening' (Nelson-Jones 1993: 87–108).

1. *Know the difference between me and you.*
   This involves trying to get inside a pupil's mind in order to understand the world from their perspective. To do this, you need to realize that just as you have a view of yourself and of the pupil, they too have their own unique view of themselves and you. For example, you might see yourself as patiently trying to encourage an uncooperative and lazy pupil to work, while they feel that you are a nagging, unreasonable teaching assistant who is trying to get them to do an impossible task.
2. *Possess an attitude of respect and acceptance.*
   We need to accept that a pupil has their own unique thoughts and feelings. We need to listen to what a pupil says with respect and without making judgements. It is important to separate our emotions from the pupil's emotions. We all bring our own emotional selves to work. For example, we might be in a bad mood because we had an argument

with our partner or our children before school, the car wouldn't start, or the central heating had packed up overnight, but whatever we are feeling it is important that we don't let our own emotional state influence how we respond to the pupils.

3. *Send good body messages.*
   We can communicate that we are listening by using positive body language. Positive body language would involve having a relaxed posture, facing the pupil, leaning slightly forward, maintaining eye contact and using appropriate facial expressions. When talking to a young child we might get down to their level. It is also important to respect a pupil's personal space because getting physically too close may be seen as threatening.

4. *Send good voice messages.*
   It is important that we are aware of aspects of our voice. *Volume* refers to how quietly or loudly we are talking. A very loud voice can overwhelm or frighten, while a very quiet voice could lead the pupil to think the teaching assistant was lacking in confidence. *Pitch* is how high or low our voice sounds. A very high-pitched voice might indicate anxiety. *Articulation* refers to how clearly we are speaking. It is important that what we say is clearly heard by the pupil. *Emphasis* refers to how expressive our voice is. Too much emphasis on words and we might come across as a would-be actor, while too little emphasis and we might come across as being cold. However, the right amount of emphasis can reflect emotion back to the pupil.

5. *Use openers, small rewards and open-ended questions.*
   Openers give pupils permission to talk and tell them you are prepared to listen. For example, you might ask, 'You seem upset. Are you all right?' Small rewards are brief verbal and non-verbal responses that you give to the pupils that tell them that you are listening and are interested in what they have to say. Examples of small rewards are nods, raised eyebrows, good eye contact and soothing voice sounds such as 'uh-hmm'. Open-ended questions encourage the pupil to keep talking. (For further information on questions, see pages 75–80.)

6. *Reword.*
   Rewording involves listening to the content of what the pupil has said and rewording or rephrasing what they have said back to them. This strategy has many advantages: it clarifies what the pupil has said; it shows them that you are listening; and perhaps it helps the pupil understand what they are trying to say. For example, if a pupil complains: 'I can't do it . . . just can't do it!', then a teaching assistant could reword this as: 'So you can't do your homework.'

7. *Reflect feelings.*
   Reflecting feelings involves not only listening to what the pupil says but also observing *how* the pupil says what they do. In particular, you are looking for a mismatch between what they say and how they say it. For example, a pupil might say they are fine but there are tears in their eyes. In this scenario, you could reflect feelings back to the pupil by saying: 'You say you are fine, but there are tears in your eyes. Perhaps you are trying to be brave?'

8. *Reflect feelings and reasons.*
   Reflect back to the pupil not only their feelings but also the reason for their feelings. This strategy can show to the pupil that you do understand them. For example, when a pupil complains to you about their teacher: 'She's so unfair. Sam didn't do his homework and he didn't get a detention', then you might reflect back the reason for their anger: 'You're angry with the teacher because she gave you a detention but not Sam?'

9. *Avoid unrewarding 'don'ts'.*
   The listener should avoid the following pitfalls:

   - Don't take control of the conversation.
   - Don't judge or moralize.
   - Don't dismiss the pupil's emotions or worries by simply reassuring them that it will turn out all right.
   - Don't assign blame, e.g. 'Well, it's all your own fault.'
   - Don't fake attention.
   - Don't put time restrictions on the conversation, e.g. 'Well, I only have five minutes, so we better make this quick.'

10. *Avoid poor thinking skills.*
    To be an effective listener you need to think about how you respond to a pupil, bearing in mind all the above points.

While these strategies are designed to help you communicate with pupils, there will be times when, from what the pupil says, it is obvious that they need to talk to someone who is professionally skilled. Even so, developing strategies that underlie active listening will help you in the everyday conversations you have with pupils. Active listening is a skill, so perhaps an example of how a teaching assistant could use these strategies would be helpful at this point.

Case study 6.1

Active listening

I work supporting Dave in a number of classes. Dave had not handed in homework since the term began and now he was being given a detention for every piece of homework missed. I just happened to bump into Dave as the final bell had gone and asked him where he was going. Dave said briefly that he had a detention to go to for not handing in his history homework. I asked him if he had any problems with his homework that prevented him from handing in his homework. Dave said no, but wouldn't look me in the eye and seemed very uncomfortable. I suggested that perhaps instead of going to the detention he might rather go with me to the learning support unit where we could talk in private about his homework. Dave looked pleased and said yes. I told him to go to the learning support unit while I checked with his history teacher if this would be all right. The history teacher thought it was a good idea, so I went back to the learning support unit to talk with Dave. Dave seemed pleased to see me and relieved that he did not have to go to the detention. I asked him if he was all right as he seemed a bit fed up. Dave mumbled that he was fed up with spending every day in detention. I told him that I would be fed up if I was him. I asked Dave again why he didn't do his homework and if there was some sort of problem. He said no, but looked very upset and again would not look me in the eye. I leaned forward, caught his eye and said that I was concerned that by not doing his homework he was getting into lots of trouble and that there must be some reason. Dave looked up and said tearfully that 'it was too hard'. I said, 'So you are not doing your homework because you are finding it too difficult?' Dave said that he didn't understand what the teacher wanted him to do, and even when he did know, he didn't know how to begin. I said, 'It must be very difficult to do homework if you don't know what to do and where to begin', and then I asked Dave if there was anyone at home to help him. Dave said that Mum used to help, but that Nanny had just had a stroke and had moved in with them and that now, when he went home, he was expected to help with the younger children. I told Dave that we would go through the homework together in the classes that I was in with him, and that, with his permission, I would talk to his teachers. I then suggested that instead of going to detention every day, he should join the school's homework club and they would help him complete his work. When Dave left the unit he was much happier.

Four levels of listening

Starr (2008: 86) describes four levels of listening:

1. *Cosmetic listening.* It appears like you are listening but really you are not; you are just pretending to listen.
2. *Conversational listening.* You are engaged in the conversation. You are listening, talking, thinking, talking and listening – but perhaps time spent on thinking about what you want to say prevents you from totally focusing on what the other person is saying.
3. *Active listening.* You are very focused on what the other person is saying. You are consciously paying attention, trying to remember what they have said and perhaps writing notes down.
4. *Deep listening.* You are more focused on the other person than yourself. This involves really getting a sense of who the other person is.

Thinking deeply

In your conversations with pupils, what type of listening do you use?
How do you move from cosmetic listening to deep listening?

Interpreting non-verbal communication

As case study 6.1 shows, we not only communicate with words but we also communicate through eye contact, tone of voice and body movements. To communicate effectively, we need to be aware of both our own and others' methods of **non-verbal communication** (see Table 6.1). Hayes (1984) says non-verbal communication (NVC) is important because it:

- adds emphasis to what we are saying
- is a form of feedback; it tells others what we are thinking and feeling, and
- tells us a lot about a person's attitude.

Moreover, when there is a conflict between what a person says and the manner in which it is said, people will attach more significance to *how* it is said. In this case, non-verbal communication is seen as a better indicator of what a person is truly thinking and feeling (Hayes 1984). In particular, as much NVC is done very quickly and without thought, we need to be aware of our non-verbal communication.

Table 6.1 Non-verbal communication

Type	Interpreting signals	How to demonstrate value and interest through body language
Posture	Sitting or standing upright and looking directly at the other person indicates that we are interested in what that other person has to say. Slouching, facing another direction and not maintaining eye contact indicates that we are bored or just not interested in what the other person has to say.	Maintain an upright body posture and maintain eye contact.
Eye contact	Generally maintaining eye contact indicates interest in the other person whereas gazing around the room indicates that we are not interested. Analysis of conversations indicates that we maintain eye contact with the other person when we start a conversation. Afterwards we might gaze away but re-engage eye contact when we want to emphasize a point or to indicate that we have stopped talking and now it is their turn to speak.	Use eye contact to indicate interest, to emphasize a point and as a cue to the other person that it is their turn to talk.
Gestures, body movements and facial expressions	Gestures such as nods and small sounds indicate your approval and that you are listening. From a very early age children can recognize and understand the meanings behind facial expressions. There are believed to be seven main types of facial expression: happiness, surprise, fear, anger, sadness, disgust and interest. When we are listening to someone we tend to mirror their facial expressions. Thus if the speaker seems upset and worried, we tend to adopt a concerned and worried expression. This strategy demonstrates empathy, i.e. it shows the other person that we are listening and concerned. Tensing of muscles and trembling twitching hands could indicate rage or fear.	Make use of gestures, such as nods and small sounds that indicate approval. Mirror facial expressions. Use appropriate facial expressions.

Basic principles of working with groups

Stages in the development of groups

Tuckman and Jensen (1977) outlined five stages of group development. These are:

1. *Forming.* When the group has just met or has been just put together, they are not properly a group but a collection of individuals. At this stage the group begins to get to know each other and set ground rules for ways of working.
2. *Storming.* At this stage a group may experience conflict as they try to work out ways of working together. There could be arguments regarding what is done, how it is done and who does what. For example, pupils might argue about who is in charge.
3. *Norming.* The group decides or agrees on ways of working. Once these have been established, then the group can get on with the task of working together.
4. *Performing.* The group gets down to work. Groups will differ on how long it takes them to get to this stage. The degree to which groups work effectively together depends on how suitable and realistic their working plans are. If new difficulties emerge, then the group might go back to the storming stage where they argue about how they are going to resolve these difficulties.
5. *Adjourning.* The task has been completed and the group prepares to disband. At this stage there may be reflection or evaluation on how they worked together. If the group has worked well both academically and socially, the group could be upset at this stage. On the other hand, if the group never managed to get on, the end will come as a relief and possibly lead to angry confrontations where group members blame each other. This means that the way groups end needs to be managed (Leadbetter *et al.* 1999).

This is a very interesting model of group development and what it highlights is just how challenging it is to get a group of pupils to work effectively together.

Areas where tension can develop

Encouraging groups to work effectively can be difficult. The first step in encouraging effective group work is to be aware of any specific issues and possible areas of conflict. Cohen *et al.* (1988) said possible issues and signs of conflict to look out for include:

- *Relationships.* Do group members spend more time arguing rather than working together? Or do some members get on *too* well and consequently other members feel left out?
- *Division of work.* Who does what? Who defines equal participation? Often groups spend time arguing over who does what. It is important to consider who assigns tasks. Does the group work this out together? Does the group pick a leader who assigns tasks? Does the teacher or teaching assistant set tasks or do they only intervene when it becomes apparent that the group cannot decide this for themselves? Groups are often concerned that everyone does their fair share of work. Possible problems could occur when there is an unfair division of work. The 'free rider effect' describes a situation where the less able pupils opt out and let the more able pupils do all the work. The 'sucker effect' refers to the situation where the more able pupils become less involved because they feel that they are being taken advantage of. On the other hand, the 'ganging up on the task' effect involves the entire group, or most

Figure 13 As Todd explained to his younger brother, being in charge is all about delegating!

of the group, deciding that they don't want to do the task (Bennett and Dunne 1992).

- *Ways of listening, communicating.* Do the individual members of the group know how to listen to each other? Do all members of the group contribute to group discussions equally? Do some members dominate the group while others are silent? Are all comments made by group members received with respect?
- *Understanding and acceptance of group goals.* Does the group understand what they should be doing? If the group does understand what they should be doing, are they willing to do the task?
- *Handling disagreements.* Who resolves group disagreements? Are the disagreements handled in a calm and reasoned manner, or does the disagreement quickly turn into a 'slanging match'? Can the group handle this by themselves, or does the teacher or teaching assistant need to intervene?

Another possible area of tension results when a teaching assistant is required to support both an individual within a group and the group itself. If a pupil has extensive needs, a teaching assistant might find it difficult to meet both the needs of the individual pupil and the demands and requests for help from the rest of the group.

Now that we have mentioned many possible problems, we need to examine how we can resolve these issues. In the next section we talk about group dynamics, specifically highlighting strategies that help groups work together effectively.

Group dynamics and ways of resolving tensions in groups

Group dynamics explain how groups work together. Much research has been conducted on the conditions that make for effective groups or teams. Effective teams should:

- have clearly defined roles and responsibilities
- agree on team and personal objectives
- encourage the involvement and participation of all team members, and
- have clear and established ways of communicating with each other.

When pupils work in groups, the first step that a teacher or a teaching assistant could take is to establish ground rules for talking and listening. In one study, groups of Year 2 pupils were asked to come up with between six and ten rules for working together. The groups suggested such ideas as 'Don't be rude', 'Keep trying', 'Have ideas', 'Don't keep comments to yourself' and 'Help each other' (National Oracy Project 1990). Such ground rules can help create a positive working atmosphere.

Other ideas for training pupils in group-work skills involve giving pupils training in cooperation, self-monitoring and self-evaluation. Training in cooperation starts with concepts of how to get on with each other, as shown in the example of establishing ground rules. Training then moves on to giving the pupils tasks where they have to learn how to work together in a positive and helpful manner. Kagan (1988) suggests assigning a task of colouring a group mural. The catch is that each pupil is allowed to use only one colour. This activity would involve the pupils working together to decide how they are going to complete this activity.

The next aspect of group work is **self-monitoring**, where each pupil is encouraged to monitor how they are doing and how the group is doing. As well as measuring progress on the task, they could also be encouraged to think about how they are getting on at a social level, i.e. how well they are listening and supporting each other.

The last aspect is **self-evaluation**. This takes place after the task is completed and has the group answer questions such as:

- Were all participants equally involved?
- How well did team members listen to and support each other?
- How were decisions made?
- What were the difficulties in working together and how were they resolved?
- What positive behaviours were seen in the group?
- Could the group have worked more effectively together? If so, how?

Of course while these ideas will help groups, there will be times when a teacher or teaching assistant needs to intervene. Sometimes a group will need help in understanding what the task is. Sometimes they will need help in setting ground rules and help in resolving disagreements positively. The key here is to give the group ideas or ways of helping themselves. When trying to balance individual and group needs, sometimes it is helpful to work with the least able and get them started and then turn to the rest of the group.

Case study 6.2

Helping a group resolve tensions

Mike, a teaching assistant, was working in a special school and was coaching the Year 5 football team. It was the first match of the year, it was half-time and they were behind by two goals. Things were not going well. Obviously the team was disappointed but what made it worse was that they were now arguing amongst themselves. Chris, who considered himself to be the real captain, was slagging off the goalie, saying that he was absolute rubbish and that so was the rest of the team. The goalie looked like he was either going to burst into tears or hit Chris. Mike took the team into the changing room and sat them all down in a circle. He said that he would ask them each in turn to make one suggestion that would lead to them playing better together. He said that they would each have their turn, and that no one would speak out of turn and that the suggestions must be positive. Mike was surprised about how well it went. Everyone had their say. The goalie said that he didn't want to be goalie and that he was much better as a forward. Another team member said he wanted to be goalie and most of them said that they would do much better if they took time to praise each other. They went back on to the pitch a much happier team and although they didn't win, they did score a goal and were very pleased with the result.

Thinking deeply

A Year 10 GCSE textile class was divided into groups. Each group was given a brief to set up a textile business enterprise to produce a decorated cushion using printing methods based on traditional South African art. The group would be made up of three pupils, consisting of a team leader/production manager, designer and marketing officer.

In group work, such as the above example, roles can be allocated to the pupils by the teacher or teaching assistant, or the group can decide for themselves who will take on what role. In your experience of working with groups, how are roles assigned?

Is there a rationale for how roles are assigned? For example, are roles always given to those with proven expertise, i.e. does the arty pupil always get the role of the designer?

Do you think the most able pupil is always the best choice for team leader/production manager? Why or why not?

What qualities make for an effective team leader?

How do you help group members achieve their potential?

Basic principles of effective working relationships with colleagues

Many of the principles we have discussed earlier about active listening and teamwork apply just as well to working with your colleagues as to working with your pupils. This next section will look at one specific theory that suggests ways to understand and improve relationships with colleagues.

Transactional analysis and ego states

Eric Berne (1968, 1991) developed a theory called **transactional analysis**. Berne was interested in how individuals communicate. He stated that every individual has three **ego states** and that when communicating with others, an individual would talk from the perspective of one of these ego states. The three ego states are:

- *Parent.* This ego state is the voice of authority, our internalized parent. When we talk from the ego state of a parent, we tend to use words that are judgemental, critical and patronizing, such as 'Don't . . .', 'I told you . . .' and 'What did I say?'
- *Adult.* When we talk from an adult ego state, or from the perspective of an adult, we talk as a rational and thinking individual. We say things such as 'I think . . .' and 'In my opinion . . .'.
- *Child.* The child ego state is the emotional part of us. When we talk from the perspective of a child, we might talk in a baby-like voice. We might be sulky, demanding, have a tantrum or be silly.

Of course this theory gets more complicated when you realize that not only do you have the option of talking from one of three ego states, but the person you are talking to has the option of responding from one of three ego states. If you think about all the conversations you have in a day, you will realize that you use many ego states depending on the situation you are in and the person to whom you are talking.

Case study 6.3

Talking from different ego states

Jane, a teaching assistant, is working on a computer with a pupil. Nothing is going right: the computer has just crashed and all the pupil's work has been lost. Jane goes frantically up to the teacher: 'I am in a total muddle with the computer. It has just crashed and I don't know what to do next!' (Jane is talking from a child ego state to the teacher's parent ego state.)

The teacher replies, 'Don't worry. I'll come over and sort it out right now.' (The teacher is talking from a parent ego state to Jane's child ego state.)

Later on in the same day

Jane (TA):   Sam is having some difficulties with his reading book. Although he is still having some difficulties with the words, I think he is getting bored and frustrated. Perhaps it would be helpful to move him on to a different book.

Teacher: I think that is a good idea. What do you think if we try him on . . . ?

Here both the teaching assistant and the teacher are communicating on an adult to adult level, i.e. they are both talking and responding from an adult ego state.

This theory comes in useful when trying to understand conversations that are difficult. Sometimes the difficulty lies in the fact that the person is talking to us in a format or way that we do not wish to be talked to.

Case study 6.4

Talking from inappropriate ego states

Jody is working in a Year 7 science class supporting two pupils who have difficulty with reading and writing. Jody sits with these pupils and sees her task as repeating instructions, as the pupils don't always follow what the teacher is saying. Sometimes Jody will act as a scribe and will copy down notes for them. After one class, the teacher called Jody over.

Teacher: Jody, you know that when I am talking in class, I like the class to be completely quiet. Now I have noticed that you are often whispering to Sarah and Jason. I think that this is sending the wrong messages to the rest of the class.

Jody (rather sulkily):   What do you want me to do?

Teacher: Sit there and be quiet.

Jody: But the pupils I am supporting . . .

| *Teacher:* | Not now, I am running late for a meeting. We will have to talk later. |

Jody found this conversation difficult as she felt the teacher was not listening to her but treating her like a naughty child. In transactional terms, the teacher was in a parent ego state and talking to her as a child. Not surprisingly, Jody responded as a sulky child – but what she really wanted was to talk to the teacher and have the teacher talk to her on an adult to adult level. The next lesson Jody came early to class.

| *Jody:* | I would like to have a word with you about what we were talking about last time. Now, while I can see your point that talking to Sarah and Jason is sending the wrong messages, I also think that without some sort of feedback in class, Sarah and Jason are not going to cope with the demands of the lesson. I would like to talk over some alternative strategies where I could give Sarah and Jason feedback, but in a way that would not be disruptive to your lesson. |

Here Jody is talking to the teacher from an adult ego state to an adult ego state in the hope that the teacher will respond likewise.

In general, when working with colleagues an adult ego state to adult ego state conversation or transaction is desirable. Talking in this manner communicates respect and encourages cooperation and teamwork.

Adult to adult communication can also be used with pupils, especially older pupils. When you talk to the pupils as if they were an adult, what you are hoping is that they will respond on a similar level.

What does a collaborative relationship look like?

Good practice involves teachers and teaching assistants working collaboratively. But what makes for a collaborative relationship or a good working partnership? Table 6.2 outlines some important factors and what they mean in practice.

Table 6.2 What is needed for a collaborative relationship

Factor	What is needed
Time for preparation	Shared planning time is important. Planning is ideally a two-way dialogue in which ideas, strategies and resources are shared. As a teacher plans the lesson, the lesson plan needs to be shared and discussed. A TA not only needs to know *what* is to be done but also *how* it should be done.
Effective communication and constructive feedback	Both teachers and TAs need feedback. Feedback involves trusting each other to be honest and say what works and what doesn't work. TAs need to know if 'they are doing it right' – and that they would be told if they were not.
Personal qualities	Both TAs and teachers need to feel valued and respected and work in such a way that each encourages and supports the other.
Having high expectations	Both TAs and teachers need to have high expectations for the pupils they work with. For example, one Deputy Head Teacher commented that she heard one member of staff say: 'Well, what do you expect from kids in this school?' To which she replied: 'Everything!'
Subject knowledge	TAs need to have a knowledge of how pupils learn and develop. Teachers need to be instrumental in helping TAs to develop this knowledge. For example, one teacher commented that modelling was key: 'Not only do TAs need to model appropriate behaviour to the children but they need to model the behaviour of the teacher', i.e. how the teacher works to support pupil learning and development. Discussing these strategies with the teacher will help the TA to develop their knowledge of pupil learning.

Thinking deeply

What do you think makes for a good working relationship?

How do you go about developing a good working relationship?

What behaviours or strategies have you seen the teacher using?

Have you adopted any of these behaviours and strategies and to what success?

Chapter 7

Self-esteem, motivation and independent learners

Definitions of self-esteem and self-concept

We all carry around with us an image of who we are, who we have been and the type of person we have the possibility of becoming. Psychologists have spent much time researching this area. At this point it is helpful to look at some definitions. Lawrence (1996) feels that there are three aspects of self:

- *Behaviour.* What we do; how we present ourselves to others.
- *Affect.* How we feel about ourselves.
- *Cognition.* How we think about ourselves.

Lawrence (1996) further states that **self-concept**, the entirety of who we are, the total person, can be divided into **self-image**, **ideal self** and **self-esteem**:

- *Self-image.* How an individual describes themselves in terms of physical and mental characteristics (e.g. how thin, tall, clever, artistic, gorgeous, are we?).
- *Ideal self.* What an individual would like to be or have in terms of physical and mental characteristics.
- *Self-esteem.* The difference between the self-image and the ideal self, i.e. the difference between the way we see ourselves and the way we would like to be. Whether we have a high or low self-esteem depends on our evaluation of ourselves. The greater the difference between self image and ideal self, the lower the self-esteem.

Harter (1982) talked about four areas where we could evaluate ourselves:

- *Cognitive competence.* How intelligent are we?
- *Social competence.* How popular are we?
- *Physical competence.* How good at sports or games are we?
- *General self-worth.* How good a person do we feel we are?

Factors that affect the development of self-esteem and self-concept

Our concept of self develops over time. Certainly a young baby would not have a self-concept but a fifteen-year-old would. Cooley (1902) put forward a **looking-glass theory** to explain how the self-concept develops: he believed that we look to others in order to define ourselves; thus, in a sense, our self is a reflection of 'how we think others see us'. Mead (1934), expanding on Cooley's views, stated that with time the views of how other specific people see us becomes internalized into a general view of how all other people see us. Mead also felt that the self was constantly being defined and redefined through the everyday interactions and conversations we have with others. Everyday interactions are important, because it is in these interactions that we make comparisons between ourselves and other people.

Becoming aware of how other people see us and our ability to make comparisons between ourselves and others develops with time. Preschoolers truly believe that they are the greatest and the best and this belief exists even when it is obvious that they are not (Frey and Ruble 1985). For example, a four-year-old might believe he can run as fast as a speeding bullet, even though he has just come last in the running race. However, by the age of six, children are able to make social comparisons. If you ask a child of six whether they are a good reader they might say, 'Well, Emma is better at reading than me because she is on the blue books. But I am better than Sam, because he is still on the red books.' As children become older they become increasingly attentive to social comparisons (picking up on teachers' and parents' looks and tone of voice) and more subtle in finding out how others have done.

Research has been carried out on gender differences in self-esteem and self-worth. A study by the American Association of University Women (Sadker and Sadker 1994) found that boys and girls have similar levels of self-esteem in primary and junior schools, although, in general, females drop in levels of self-esteem relative to males during secondary school. Kwa (1994) found that having a good physical appearance was the strongest predictor of self-worth in females, whereas males felt valued for how their bodies performed in athletic activities.

Social factors can influence self-concept and self-esteem. Social factors relate to the value that society places on performing certain activities, occupying certain roles or jobs and possessing certain physical traits. Society values individuals who excel at sports, gain leadership roles (e.g. head girl, head boy, captain of the football team) and possess physical attributes such as beauty. Within the last twenty years, the incidence of adolescents with eating disorders has risen dramatically. Although boys do suffer from eating disorders, females make up the majority of sufferers, with younger and younger girls becoming worried about weight. Society celebrates the supermodel and many girls aspire to this ideal.

Although we can say that English culture as a whole values certain characteristics and traits, England is now a multiracial and multi-ethnic society. Sometimes subcultures will have values that conflict with the culture at large. Juvenile gangs could be considered a subculture. Certainly respect for authority and academic excellence would not be seen as valued within these subcultures.

An important concept in this area is the issue of labelling. Rosenthal and Jacobson (1966) conducted a classic study in this area on the effects of teacher expectations and what they termed **self-fulfilling prophecies**. The researchers went into a school and gave an intelligence test to all pupils. The researchers then told the teachers that on the basis of the test results they had identified certain pupils who were 'academic bloomers', i.e. pupils who would really come on in leaps and bounds in the forthcoming academic year. At the end of the year, they went back to the school and administered another intelligence test to all the pupils. They discovered that these 'academic bloomers' had indeed increased in intelligence. However, the catch is that the researchers had lied to the teachers at the beginning of the year. There were no 'academic bloomers' – the researchers had just chosen pupils' names randomly from the school register. The important aspect of this study was that the pupils who the teachers thought would improve academically did. Why did this happen? Perhaps the pupils improved simply because the teachers thought they would. Perhaps the teachers spent more time with these pupils. Perhaps the teachers encouraged them and praised them more. But what this study does show is the power of teacher expectations and that pupils can live up to (as in this study) or down to these expectations.

Strategies that will enhance self-esteem

What has been said in the previous section has important implications for working with pupils in schools. There are several key points:

- Pupils develop a self-concept through their interactions with others. In terms of a school environment, this includes other pupils and the teaching staff.
- Pupils will observe how others see them and react by internalizing this into a view regarding how 'others think of me'. So, if others see me as thick and naughty, in time that is how I see myself.
- Pupils will draw social comparisons between themselves and other pupils.
- As they grow older, pupils become very good at picking up subtle clues in social interactions. Pupils will pick up on tone of voice, the use of sarcasm, various looks, etc.

What all this means is that a teaching assistant needs to be aware of damaging interactions between pupils. Moreover, in order to boost a pupil's self-esteem, they must always be aware of how they themselves are reacting to the pupil.

General strategies for interacting with pupils are:

- Try to think positively about all the pupils you work with. Try to deal with even the difficult pupils in a positive manner.
- Make a point of telling the pupils what their strengths are.
- Communicate to the pupil that you like them and value them.
- Praise pupils regularly but ensure that the praise is genuine.
- Give them tasks that they can succeed in.
- If they don't succeed in the whole task, find some aspect of the task that they have done well.
- Tell the pupil about your mistakes. Tell them how you have learned through your mistakes. Tell them how you felt when you failed at something. Tell them how you dealt with failure by trying harder. Tell them we all make mistakes and that mistakes are an important part of the learning process.
- Encourage pupils to be supportive of each other.

Of course these suggestions sound good, but how do you do it in the real classroom environment? Imagine the scene described in case study 7.1.

Case study 7.1

The student who won't start work

Everyone in the Year 9 math class is settling down to do their work – except for James. James is slouched in his chair; he has not brought in his math textbook or his workbook, nor does he have any pens or paper. James looks bored and defiant and is chewing gum noisily. The teaching assistant has given him some paper and a pen yet he has still not started to work even though she has asked him twice.

Thinking deeply

Below are three possible responses the teaching assistant in case study 7.1 could give James:

1. 'James, I have had enough of you. You never bring in your books. You will never pass your exams at this rate and as for your chewing gum, well, that's about the only thing you can do.'
2. 'James, if you are not going to work, then I'll go and help someone else who is.'
3. 'James, you have the ability to be clever, but you need to try. Why are you still just sitting there? If you don't know where to begin you know, you just have to ask me.'

Which response do you think you would give?

Which response would be the most constructive for and respectful to James?

However, despite you doing all you can to encourage an atmosphere of respect and reminding pupils of the school behaviour charter, pupils can be very cruel to each other at times. Sometimes in these cases it is recommended that you work with the pupils to develop an internal sense of self-worth. For example, one activity (Canfield 1994) has the teacher instruct the pupils to learn by heart the following phrase: 'No matter what you say or do to me, I am still a worthwhile person.'

The relationship between self-esteem and achievement

Branden (1984: 4) argues that self-esteem has profound consequences on every aspect of our lives. Other researchers have found that those pupils with high self-esteem do better at school than those with low self-esteem (Davies and Brember 1999). However, the relationship between self-esteem and achievement is complex; doing well increases self-esteem but increases in self-esteem do not necessarily result in improvements in performance or achievement. This can be explained in terms of the pupil's internal dialogue, i.e. what they say to themselves. Remember that our beliefs about ourselves are formed by internalizing comments that others say about us. If a pupil hears from others that they are brilliant, great, fantastic, etc., this may result in them believing that they are brilliant and therefore feeling really good about themselves. However, for high self-esteem to influence academic behaviour, the pupil needs to make a connection between what they do (their actions) and what happens to them (the consequences of their actions). So ideally those supporting teaching and learning want pupils to make connections between effort and ability. They would like pupils to say: 'I studied really hard and I achieved a really good grade and now I feel really good about myself!' Therefore, consideration needs to be given to how we give out praise.

Thinking deeply

Evaluate the following praise statements by completing this table:

Praise Statement	How does this statement make the pupil feel? Does it raise their self-esteem?	What does this statement tell the pupil about the relationship between ability and effort?	How will this statement affect the future behaviour of the pupil?
You are great!!			
Wow! You are a star!!			
You are really putting a lot of effort into this!			
You are getting smart because of your hard work!			

Praise Statement	How does this statement make the pupil feel? Does it raise their self-esteem?	What does this statement tell the pupil about the relationship between ability and effort?	How will this statement affect the future behaviour of the pupil?
That's correct: that means you tried hard.			
That is the wrong answer; that means you should have tried harder.			

Source: Siegel Robertson (2000)

Thinking deeply

What is the relationship between ability and effort?
How would *you* answer the following questions?
How would *your* pupils answer the following questions?
What does it mean to be *clever*?
What does it mean to be someone who *learns easily*?
What does it mean to be someone who finds it *difficult to learn*?
What do pupils who find *learning easy* do when they get stuck?
What do pupils who find *learning difficult* do when they get stuck?
What would a pupil who finds *learning easy* do if they made a mistake?
What would a pupil who finds *learning difficult* do if they made a mistake?

Motivation

Well-motivated pupils are a joy to teach. When pupils are eager to learn, the job of those supporting teaching and learning is so much easier. But what is motivation? Motivation can be described as a drive that pushes a person towards a goal, or a force that energizes a person to act. Dornyei (2001: 8) states that motivation accounts for:

- why people decide to do something
- how long they are willing to sustain the activity, and
- how hard they are going to pursue it.

Specifically, motivation to learn involves the choice to engage in an activity, the persistence to stay on task and the effort expended on that activity.

Thinking deeply

What motivates you?
How do you motivate others?
What does a motivated pupil, group or class look like? (i.e. can you tell whether they are motivated by their actions?).

Central to the discussion of motivation is the distinction between intrinsic and extrinsic motivation. Extrinsic motivation involves performing an activity as a means to an end, i.e. as a way to receive some external reward. Examples of external rewards could be grades, merit points or stars. External rewards are important and beneficial because they can encourage appropriate behaviour for learning, but they do not by themselves create pupils who are independent learners. On the other hand, intrinsic motivation involves motivation for the behaviour being controlled by internal thought processes and desires rather than external rewards. A pupil who is intrinsically motivated engages in an activity out of an internal desire to learn and develop. Strategies to encourage intrinsically motivated pupils include emphasizing the relevance of the activity, creating curiosity, engaging the learner by providing a variety of practical activities and games, matching teaching styles to learning styles, and allowing pupils to set personal goals

Figure 14 Dylan, at the age of 5, knew that with enough practice he could be a master of the sack race, the hula-hoop race and, not to forget, the egg and spoon race.

and develop their own plans of action (Stipek 1988). Research suggests that intrinsic motivation can improve a pupil's school achievement as significantly as an additional 20–25 IQ points (Haywood 2004). This relates to the role that engagement, persistence and effort have on ability. Daniel

Table 7.1 Characteristics of fixed and growth mindsets

	Fixed mindset	Growth mindset
How important is it to look smart?	These pupils worry about how smart they are and what others will think of them. This anxiety can lead pupils to avoiding learning opportunities that appear too challenging in case they fail.	These pupils are more interested in learning rather than looking smart. These pupils are open to learning challenges.
What is the relationship between effort and ability?	These pupils believe that if you have ability then you don't need to work as knowledge would just come. If you do have to work, then this would mean that you didn't have the ability in the first place.	Pupils believe that working harder makes you smarter. Therefore effort increases ability.
How are setbacks and mistakes perceived?	If a pupil makes a mistake or has a setback they are likely to question whether they are in fact clever. These pupils see mistakes as a reflection of lack of ability.	If a pupil makes a mistake or has a setback then this is a signal for the pupil to try harder or to use another strategy.
When do you feel clever?	These pupils will state that they feel clever when they find something easy, they finish a task quickly without a mistake or when other pupils can't do what they can.	These pupils say that they feel clever when they have had to really struggle to learn, when they realize that through their effort they have made progress and when they have helped others to learn.
How motivated are these pupils?	Motivation to take on learning challenges is limited as these pupils believe ability is fixed and effort has no role to play.	Motivation to take on and persist with learning challenges is high due to pupils' belief that achievement is related to effort.

Source: Dweck (2000, 2008a and b)

Coyle, in his 2009 book *The Talent Code*, states that anyone can become talented if they are sufficiently motivated, practise and are guided by a master coach. Shenk (2010b) put the amount of practice necessary to become an expert as 10,000 hours.

This emphasis on effort and practice relates to Carol Dweck's (2000, 2008) concept of fixed and growth mindsets. Fixed and growth mindsets relate to beliefs that individuals have about how intelligence develops. Carol Dweck argues that these mindsets have a profound impact on individuals' motivation, learning and achievement. Table 7.1 describes the characteristic of individuals with fixed or growth mindsets.

The implication is that those pupils who have a fixed mindset have set a self-imposed limit on what they can achieve. To maximize potential, those supporting teaching and learning need to encourage a growth mindset in the pupils with whom they work. Dweck (2000, 2008) attributes the development of a fixed mindset to well intentioned praise that fails to make the connection between ability and effort. Praising children and pupils is important, but praise needs to be considered – pupils need to develop a positive approach to learning that recognizes the connection between ability and effort and that sees mistakes and setbacks as an important part of the learning process. (For further information on praise, see pages 183–4.)

Thinking deeply

What would you say to a pupil who says: 'Look at him – he's got an A in his exam but that's only because he studied. He's not really clever.'?

Case study 7.2

Fixed and growth mindsets

Daphne worked with two groups in her classroom. She found there were surprising differences between them.

The *less able group*, although quite noisy, were always eager to solve a problem or a challenge and would usually work at the task until they did so. If needed, this group would ask for help and they would not get fazed by mistakes or setbacks. Daphne reflected that maybe this was because the pupils often made mistakes and now had realized that mistakes were just a signal to try harder or try something different.

On the other hand, the *able group* were more focused and often managed to accomplish their work with ease. However, Daphne commented that as a group they got overwhelmed when they came up against something that they could not do. Daphne reflected that both as a group and individually they seldom made mistakes.

Daphne decided to question the groups about what they thought was the relationship between ability and effort. (For further information on this relationship, see pages 185–7.) Their responses were interesting:

- The able group said that pupils who find it easy to learn do not need to ask for assistance or help and that those who find it easy to learn would not get stuck or make mistakes.
- The less able group, although saying that they did not find learning easy, knew a number of strategies to use when they made a mistake or got stuck. As a group they seem to realize that making mistakes were part of the learning process.

Thinking deeply

How does an understanding of fixed and growth mindsets help explain the different attitudes of the able and less able group in case study 7.2? What should Daphne do?

Factors that promote independence

The ultimate aim of an education system is to give the pupil a thirst for acquiring knowledge and the necessary skills in order to do so. This view sees learning as a lifelong process. While learning is very much guided by the teaching staff in the early years, it is expected that pupils going on to college and university will have become independent learners. Independent learners:

- know what they need to do in order to complete the assignment or answer the question
- know how to ask for help
- know how to gather the needed information
- know how to present ideas
- know how to use their time effectively
- know how to review and evaluate their own work against what they have been asked to achieve, and
- take responsibility for their learning.

It is obvious that these skills are of value. But how are they learned? Some pupils will naturally pick these skills up, while others will need to be taught these skills in a step-by-step approach.

Strategies designed to encourage independence

Independent learning can be encouraged by:

- Encouraging choice and decision-making skills, which create in the pupil a sense of ownership, responsibility and pride in their work.
- Specific study skills programmes that aim to teach pupils how to study effectively and so give pupils the skills to become independent learners. One such programme that we have talked about is process-based instruction. This programme teaches skills such as where to start, what actions are needed, how to monitor work and how to review or verify whether work has been completed. (For further information on process-based instruction, see pages 84–6.) Another programme is Robinson's SQ3R method of effective reading.

Robinson's SQ3R method of effective reading

This method is ideally suited to older pupils who will use textbooks and other reading resources for research purposes. The steps in this method are:

1. *Survey.* Before reading the chapter, try to get an overview of what material the chapter is presenting. Looking at chapter outlines and various headings in the text will help.
2. *Question.* Convert every heading in the text into a question. Asking questions helps you become involved in the learning process.
3. *Read.* Read one section of the text at a time with the goal of answering the question.
4. *Recite.* After reading the section, answer in your own words the question you have formed. Sometimes it is helpful to do this out loud. At this point you could make some notes.
5. *Review.* When you have finished the chapter, review the key notes you have made.

Teaching choice and decision-making skills

Before we go any further it is important to define our terms. What do we mean by choice and decision making? *Choice* has been defined as the act of making a selection of a preferred alternative from among several options (Shevin and Klein 1984). So a choice involves selecting an option from several possibilities. *Decision making* is defined as a process which involves a reasonable amount of thinking that is focused on deciding what to believe and do (Ennis 1987). In this book we have previously talked about making the pupil aware that they have choices regarding how they behave. But what other decisions and choices do pupils have?

- Pupils can choose what books to read.
- Pupils can choose what resources they want to use. A pupil at a primary level working on a maths worksheet might have a choice between using a number line or counters.
- Pupils might be given a choice in regard to what to do for a project, an essay or coursework.
- Pupils can choose to go to homework club.
- Pupils can select what extra activity clubs they join.

So how can a teacher or teaching assistant encourage or facilitate choice and decision-making opportunities for their pupils? The following suggestions have been seen to be helpful:

- Give pupils realistic choices.
- To be able to make a choice, the pupils need to know what the options are and to have some sort of experience of what the options involve. For example, a pupil cannot realistically make a choice to attend a homework club if they do not know what a homework club entails.
- Do not give too many choices, because this can overwhelm the pupils.
- Support and respect the choices and decisions that pupils have made.
- Help pupils to evaluate their choices and decisions by asking questions.

When considering giving choices and allowing pupils to make decisions, the question most teachers and teaching assistants have is: 'What do I do when the pupil does not make the 'right' choice?'

Thinking deeply

Scenario 1
Judy, a teaching assistant in a junior school, supports Dan, who has difficulties in reading and spelling. Every week Dan can choose a book that he can read with the teaching assistant. What Judy has noticed is that every week Dan always goes for the easy option – Dan always chooses books that he can read easily. Therefore his choice does not extend his reading abilities.

Scenario 2
Nancy, a teaching assistant, works in a secondary school. On this day, the teacher had asked the class to write a poem on 'Rain', and Nancy had to go around the class and help any pupils who were having problems. Nancy recalls:
'I was very impressed with the children's work. I stopped and read Robert's poem. It was lovely. I said to Robert: "What a lovely poem!" but instead of being pleased he said "No it's not" and proceeded to rip the paper up.'

Scenario 3
Joe is a teaching assistant working in a primary school. He states:
'I was supporting a number of pupils in a math class. At the end of the lesson I was going around the class quickly checking pupils' work. I looked at Amy's worksheet. I noticed that there were many mistakes. I said to Amy, "Shall we check this over together?" Amy said, "There is no need! I am brilliant at maths!"'

What should the teaching assistant do in each of these scenarios?
Does the research on choices, self-esteem or mindsets suggest possible ways forward?

Glossary

The first occurrence of each of these terms is highlighted by bold in the main text.

Accommodation is the term used by Piaget to describe how individuals change or modify schemas to incorporate new experiences.

Active listening is a special type of listening where we communicate to the person with whom we are talking that we have indeed heard and understood what they have said.

Adaptation, according to Piaget, describes the changes an individual makes in response to the environment. The changes involve the development of schemas through the processes of assimilation and accommodation.

ADHD or Attention Deficit Hyperactivity Disorder is a condition marked by excessive activity, impulsiveness and problems in sustained attention.

Assimilation is the term used by Piaget to describe how new information is fitted into existing schemas.

Auditory learners prefer to learn through hearing and listening to material.

Autism Spectrum Conditions are characterized by problems in social interaction, communication and imaginative activity, combined with a limited range of activities and interests. Autism is now commonly referred to as Autism Spectrum Conditions (ASC).

Basic interpersonal communication skills is the level of language first learned by toddlers and preschoolers. In acquiring a second language, it is thought to take from one to two years to achieve this level of competence.

Behavioural analysis is the process of trying to understand and explain a person's behaviour.

Biological maturation   describes how an individual changes and develops with age.

Bottom-up processing   involves using our knowledge of basic principles to help us process material. An example of bottom-up processing would be using the knowledge of letter/sound combinations to help us to read.

Braille   is a tactile system of communication consisting of raised dots corresponding to letters of the alphabet. This system is used by individuals with sensory impairment.

Classical conditioning   involves associating the automatic reactions caused by one event to other events that just happen to be occurring at the same time.

Cochlear implants   are a type of hearing aid that relies on sending electrical signals directly to the auditory nerve to provide a sense of hearing.

Cognitive academic language proficiency   is the language used within classroom contexts and the standard necessary to cope with GCSEs. In acquiring a second language, it is thought to take from five to seven years to achieve this level of competence.

Cognitive development   is the development of intellectual processes to include thinking, knowing, reasoning, understanding and problem solving.

Cognitive disequilibrium   is an unpleasant mental state that results when an individual realizes that they cannot fit new experiences into existing schemas. In everyday language, an individual becomes confused when they realize they don't understand.

Co-morbidity   is the degree to which one health condition is associated with another condition.

Conditioned emotional responses   is a type of learning that results in certain events and situations being associated with particular emotions and feelings.

Conditioned response   is the response elicited by a conditioned stimulus. The term is used in explaining the process of classical conditioning.

Conditioned stimulus   is a stimulus that initially does not elicit any reflex response, but comes to do so by being paired with an unconditioned stimulus. The term is used in explaining the process of classical conditioning.

Conserve   is a term used by Piaget to describe the child's awareness that an object will only have changed if something has been added or subtracted. Once the child has developed the ability to conserve, they will not be fooled by visual appearances.

Constructive feedback is a type of feedback that both acknowledges what has been done and what still needs to be done in a manner that is seen as helpful and positive by the individual receiving the feedback.

Critical period hypothesis is a belief held by certain theorists that the earlier a language is learnt the easier it is, and that it is easier to learn a language before puberty than after.

Decentre is a term used by Piaget to describe a child's ability to hold and understand in their mind multiple and sometimes opposing views. For example, two lumps of play-dough of the same weight still weigh the same even if they have been rolled into different shapes and no longer look the same.

Deferred imitation is the ability to imitate or copy a behaviour after a period of time has passed.

Developmental Coordination Disorder refers to problems in motor coordination experienced by a child that cannot be explained by a general medical condition. The condition is also known as Dyspraxia.

Discovery learning is an approach that sees an individual's active participation in a learning activity as being responsible for the development of new knowledge.

Down's syndrome is a chromosomal anomaly where there are forty-seven chromosomes in each cell instead of forty-six. An extra chromosome 21 is responsible for this condition.

Dyslexia is a condition where people have difficulty learning to read and spell despite adequate intelligence, instruct ion and opportunity.

Dyspraxia is a condition marked by problems with motor coordination. Dyspraxia is also known as Developmental Coordination Disorder.

Echolalia is a condition where an individual repeats words or phrases that they heard others say; however, this repetition is not used as a form of communication with others. This condition is often found in individuals with autism.

Egocentrism and egocentric are terms used by Piaget to describe the tendency of a young child to believe that others see things from their perspective.

Ego states is a term used by Eric Berne in his theory of transactional analysis. According to the theory, each individual has three ego states or perspectives from which they communicate to others. The three ego states are parent, adult and child.

Emotional intelligence is being aware of, managing and using one's own emotions productively. Emotional intelligence also involves the ability to read and understand others' emotions and the art of dealing effectively with all aspects of social relationships.

Encoding is the process of transforming incoming information into a form that can be stored in memory.

Expressive language is the extent to which an individual can communicate.

Fine motor skills are refined movements using only certain body parts, e.g. handwriting.

Gaze monitoring is the ability to follow another person's gaze, i.e. the ability to know what another person is looking at.

General symbolic function, according to Piaget, is one of the main accomplishments of the sensori-motor stage of development. This accomplishment includes the development of language, deferred imitation and make-believe play.

Grapheme–phoneme awareness is knowing which letters or combinations of letters are associated with which sounds. (Graphemes refers to the letters of the alphabet; phonemes refers to particular sound units.)

Graphemes are a written symbol of a language system, e.g. letters of the alphabet.

Gross motor skills are physical movements that involve the whole body, e.g. jumping.

Group dynamics are the interactions that take place within a group.

Group socialization theory, as argued by Harris (1997), states that it is the social or peer group to which an individual belongs that determines their behaviour.

Holophrases are one-word sentences. It is a stage in early language development where one word is used in combination with gestures to communicate the meaning.

Hyperlexia is a condition where a child's reading skills greatly surpass their comprehension skills, i.e. an individual can fluently read a passage of text but not understand what they have just read.

Hypothetical deductive reasoning is a type of reasoning that emerges in Piaget's formal operational stage. Individuals of 11 and above have an understanding of hypotheses, which involves creating, noting implications, testing, drawing conclusions and, from the analysis of conclusions, creating yet more hypotheses.

Ideal self is the person who we would like to be, i.e. the physical and mental characteristics we would like to have.

Ideational is a type of dyspraxia where individuals have difficulty in planning a sequence of coordinated movements.

Ideo-motor is a type of dyspraxia where individuals know what they want to do and what the right sequence of movements is, but have difficulties in executing these movements. These individuals may appear clumsy or awkward.

Intelligence tests are administered by an educational or clinical psychologist to measure cognitive or intellectual ability.

Instrumental pointing is used to communicate the need to have an object. For example, a baby points to an object because they want to have that object.

Intrinsic means stemming from within the person.

Kinaesthetic learners prefer to learn through physical movement and hands-on activities.

Language acquisition device is believed by some theorists to be 'something' within our brain that we are born with, an innate mental mechanism, that allows us to develop language, specifically grammar.

Learning style is an individual's preference in how they wish to learn new information.

Looking-glass theory, developed by Cooley (1902), states that we look to others in order to define who we are.

Maturational readiness is the age or stage of development when a child will be ready and able to learn new knowledge.

Memory strategy is that 'something special' that we need to do to unrelated information in order to remember it.

Metamemory is knowledge about memory, in particular one's own memory abilities.

Moon is a tactile system of communication based on raised letters that are similar to the letters of the alphabet as we know them. This system is used with individuals with both sensory impairments and general learning disabilities.

Motherese is a style of language used by an adult when talking to a baby or young child. This language is characterized by shorter, grammatically simple sentences spoken at a higher pitch and at a slower pace.

Multi-sensory rooms are designed for individuals with multiple disabilities. Multi-sensory rooms offer the individual a range of sensory experiences involving sight, sound, touch and smell. Some of these experiences can be controlled by the individual with disabilities by the use of specially designed switches.

Multi-sensory techniques   are often used in the teaching of phonics. This technique aims to teach through an approach that uses all senses: auditory, visual and kinaesthetic.

Non-verbal communication involves communication with others through the use of eye contact, tone of voice and body movements.

Objects of reference   are specific objects that have a meaning assigned to them. Objects of reference are used as a system of communication with individuals who have multiple disabilities.

Object permanence   is a term used by Piaget to describe the realization that objects continue to exist in time and space regardless of whether an individual can see them or not.

Occupational therapists   are involved in the assessment and treatment of disorders of movement. Occupational therapists assess what daily living skills an individual has and can provide suitable equipment and adaptations to the individual's environment so that they can be as independent as possible.

Over-regularization/Over-generalization   is a stage in early grammar development where the child will apply known existing rules of grammar to all words; at this stage the child will not know that certain words are exceptions to the rule. For example, a child at this stage might say: 'I hurted'.

Perceptual style   is how pupils take in and process information, specifically what senses are being used. Pupils will show preferences in what senses they use to process information. (See visual learners, auditory learners and kinaesthetic learners.)

Phonemes   are distinct sound units, which in combination form words.

Physiotherapists   are involved in the assessment and treatment of disorders of movement. Physiotherapists use treatments such as exercise, heat and manipulation.

Picture Exchange Communication System (PECS)   is an intervention used with individuals who have difficulties with language and communication. This system uses picture cards that represent objects. To begin with, a pupil is required to exchange a picture of a desired object for the object itself. The system then encourages an individual to communicate by creating combinations of pictures corresponding to sentences.

Probes   are follow-up questions designed to elicit more specific information.

Process-based instruction   is a strategy devised by Ashman and

Conway (1993) that teaches pupils how to solve problems and plan their work.

Prompts are follow-up questions given to a pupil when the initial answer received is not quite the answer you are looking for. The aim of a prompt is to help the pupil give the desired answer.

Proprioceptive system sends information to the brain through receptors present in the muscles and joints that enable an individual to be aware of body position and to move without visual guidance.

Prosopagnosia is a rare condition where individuals have no problem seeing faces, but have difficulties making sense of faces. An individual with such a condition could meet a close relative on the street and not recognize them.

Proto-declarative pointing is used by babies to communicate. This pointing is not based on a desire to have an object but more a desire to share an experience.

Receptive language is how much an individual can understand of what is being said to them.

Repetitive routines are daily events in a child's life, e.g. getting dressed or having a bath. In the course of these repetitive routines, parents often use the same language. This repetition of the same language in the same context helps the child to break the code of language.

Resilience factors are those situations, events, relationships and personality traits that serve to protect an individual from negative conditions such as mental health problems.

Retrieval describes the process of how we access stored information.

Risk factors are those situations, events, relationships and personality traits that increase the chances that an individual will experience negative conditions such as mental health problems.

Scaffolding is a concept used by Vygotsky and expanded upon by Bruner to describe the process of help by which a more skilled individual teaches a less skilled individual.

Schemas are organized patterns or units of action or thought that we construct to make sense of our interactions with the world.

Self-concept is defined as the whole person. Self-concept can be divided into the self-image, the ideal self and self-esteem.

Self-esteem is the extent to which one values oneself.

Self-fulfilling prophecy is the tendency for things to turn out as expected. For example, a teacher who expects a pupil to fail might treat the pupil in a manner that increases the likelihood that they will fail. In this example the teacher's expectations have come true, but the pupil's failure is in part due to the teacher's behaviour.

Self-image is how an individual describes themselves.

Self-monitoring involves the individual being aware of exactly how they are engaging in an activity.

Sequential language acquisition involves an individual first learning one language and then at some later stage being introduced to a second language.

Simultaneous language acquisition occurs when a child, from infancy, learns two languages at the same time.

Social learning theory states that we learn by observing and imitating others.

Spiral curriculum is a concept used by Bruner that sees concepts being developed and redeveloped with increasing levels of complexity as the child progresses through the education system.

Storage of information for future use occurs after the information has been encoded. According to Piaget, information is stored in units of mental thought called schemas.

Tactile receptors are specialized cells within the skin that send information about light, touch, pain, temperature and pressure to the brain.

Task analysis involves breaking a task or a skill into steps or component parts. Once the smaller steps or parts have been identified, it is possible to determine what steps or parts the pupil can do and what steps or parts they cannot do.

Telegraphic speech is a stage in early language development where the child will use only key words to express themselves.

Theory of mind is the ability to guess what other people are thinking and feeling. An individual who has this ability can use it to make sense of and predict other individuals' behaviour.

Top-down processing involves using our knowledge of the world, what happens in the world and our knowledge of spoken language to help us process material, e.g. to help us to read.

Transactional analysis is a theory developed by Eric Berne. Berne was interested in how individuals communicate with each other. From this theory Berne devised a therapy to enhance communication.

Transitivity is a type of reasoning involved in answering questions such as: 'If Joe is taller than Sam, and Sam is taller than Rob, who is tallest: Joe or Rob?'

Unconditioned response is a reflex response elicited by an unconditioned stimulus. The term is used in explaining the process of classical conditioning.

Unconditioned stimulus is a stimulus that has the natural ability to evoke a reflex response. The term is used in explaining the process of classical conditioning.

Vestibular apparatus refers to receptors that are located within the inner ear that automatically coordinate movements of the eyes, head, ears and body in order to maintain balance.

Visual learners prefer to learn through seeing and watching.

Zone of Proximal Development is a term coined by Vygotsky to describe the difference between what individuals could achieve by themselves and what they could achieve with assistance. Vygotsky saw this difference as measuring individuals' potential to learn.

Bibliography

APA (1995) *Diagnostic and Statistical Manual of Mental Disorders*, 4th edn, Washington DC: American Psychological Association
—— (2000) *Diagnostic and Statistical Manual of Mental Disorders*, 4th edn, Washington DC: American Psychological Association
Ashman, A. and Conway, R. (1993) *Using Cognitive Methods in the Classroom*, London: Routledge
Assessment Reform Group (ARG) (2002) *Assessment for Learning: 10 Principles. Research-Based Principles to Guide Classroom Practice*, available online at: http://www.assessment-reform-group.org/images/Principles%20for%20website.doc (retrieved 15 June 2010)
Atkinson, R. L., Atkinson, R. C., Smith, E. E. and Bem, D. J. (1993) *Introduction to Psychology*, 11th edn, New York: Harcourt Brace
Bagwell, C. L., Newcomb, A. F. and Bukowski, W. M. (1998) 'Preadolescent friendship and peer rejection as predictors of adult adjustment', *Child Development*, 69, 140–53
Bailey, M. (1967) 'The utility of phonic generalisations in Grades One through Six', *Reading Teacher*, 20, 413–18
Balchin, T., Hymer, B. and Matthews, D. (2009) *The Routledge International Companion to Gifted Education*, London: Routledge
Bandura, A. (1977) *Social Learning Theory*, Morristown NJ: General Learning Press
Barkley, R. A. (1998) 'Attention Deficit Hyperactivity Disorder', *Scientific American*, September, 44–9
Baron-Cohen, S., Leslie, A. M. and Frith, U. (1985) 'Does the autistic child have a "theory of mind"?' *Cognition*, 21, 37–46
Barrs, M., Ellis, S., Hester, H. and Kelly, A. V. (1988) *The Primary Language Record Handbook*, London: Centre for Literacy in Primary Education
Bell, A. W., Kuchemann, D. and Costello, J. (1983) *A Review of Research in Mathematical Education: Part A, Teaching and Learning*, Windsor: NFER-Nelson
Bennett, N. and Dunne, E. (1992) *Managing Classroom Groups*, Hemel Hempstead: Simon and Schuster

Berko Gleason, J. B. (1997) *The Development of Language*, 4th edn, Boston MA: Allyn and Bacon

Berne, E. (1968) *Games People Play*, London: Penguin Books

—— (1991) *Transactional Analysis in Psychotherapy*, London: Souvenir Press

Blatchford, P., Bassett, P., Brown, P., Koutsoubou, M., Martin, C., Russell, A., Webster, R. and Rubie-Davies, C. (2009) *Deployment and Impact of Support Staff in Schools: The Impact of Support Staff in Schools (Results from Strand 2, Wave 2)*, Research Report No DCSF-RR148, London: Institute of Education, University of London

Bondy, A. S. and Frost, L. A. (1994) 'The Picture Exchange Communication System', *Focus on Autistic Behaviour*, 9 (3), 1–19

Branden, N. (1984) *Honoring the Self: Self-Esteem and Personal Transformation*, New York: Bantam Books

British Broadcasting Corporation (BBC) (1997) *Dyslexia in the Primary Classroom*, Teaching Today series, London: BBC Education in association with British Dyslexia Association

British Stammering Association (1997) *A Chance to Speak: Helping a Pupil who Stammers: A Practical Guide for Teachers*, London: BSA

Britton, T. (2008) *Holding Open a Space*, unpublished MA(Ed) dissertation, University of Chichester

Brown, G. and Wragg, E. C. (1993) *Questioning*, London: Routledge

Bruner, J. (1963) *The Process of Education*, Cambridge MA: Harvard University Press

—— (1983) *Child's Talk: Learning to Use Language*, New York: Norton

Buckley, S. (1993) 'Language development in children with Down's syndrome: reasons for optimism', *Down's Syndrome: Research and Practice*, 1 (1), 3–9

—— (1995) 'Improving the expressive language skills of teenagers with Down's syndrome', *Down's Syndrome: Research and Practice*, 3 (3), 110–15

—— (1996) 'Reading before talking: learning about mental abilities from children with Down's syndrome', The University of Portsmouth Inaugural Lectures, 9 May 1996.

Buckley, S. and Bird, G. (1993) 'Teaching children with Down's syndrome to read', *Down's Syndrome: Research and Practice*, 1 (1), 34–9

Canfield, J. (1994) *100 Ways to Enhance Self-Concept in the Classroom: A Handbook for Teachers*, 2nd edn, Boston MA: Allyn and Bacon

Carter, R. (1998) *Mapping the Mind*, London: Weidenfeld and Nicolson

Charlton, T. and David, K. (eds) (1993) *Managing Misbehaviour in Schools*, London: Routledge

Chomsky, N. (1965) *Aspects of the Theory of Syntax*, Cambridge MA: MIT Press

Claxton, G. (1999) *Wise Up: Learning to Live the Learning Life*, Stafford: Network Education Press Ltd

Cohen, A. R., Fink, S. L, Gadon, H. and Willits, R. D. (1988) *Effective Behaviour in Organizations*, 4th edn, Homewood IL: Irwin

Collier, V. (1995) 'Acquiring a second language for school', *Directions in Language & Education National Clearinghouse for Bilingual Education*, 1 (4), Fall 1995.

Conners, C. K., Epstein, J. N., March, J. S., Angold, A., Wells, K. C., Klaric, J., Swanson, J. M., Arnold, L. E., Abikoff, H. B., Elliott, G. R., Greenhill, L. L., Hechtman, L., Hinshaw, S. P., Hoza, B., Jensen, P. S., Kraemer, H. C., Newcorn, J. H., Pelham, W. E., Severe, J. B., Vitiello, B. and Wigal, T. (2001) 'Multimodal treatment of ADHD in the MTA: an alternative outcome analysis', *Journal of the American Academy of Child and Adolescent Psychiatry*, 40, 159–67

Conrad, K., Cermak, S. A. and Drake, C. (1983) 'Differentiation of praxis among children', *American Journal of Occupational Therapy*, 37, 466–73

Cooley, C. H. (1902) *Human Nature and the Social Order*, New York: Scribner

Cousins, L. and Jennings, J. (2003) *The Positive Behaviour Handbook: The Complete Guide to Promoting Positive Behaviour in Your School*, London: PFP Publishing Ltd

Cowen, E. L., Pederson, A., Babigian, H., Izzo, L. D. and Trost, M. A. (1973) 'Long-term follow-up of early detected vulnerable children', *Journal of Consulting and Clinical Psychology*, 41, 438–46

Coyle, D. (2009) *The Talent Code: Greatness Isn't Born. It's Grown. Here's How*, New York: Bantam

Critchley, M. (1970) *The Dyslexic Child*, Springfield IL: Thomas

Cummins, J. (1984) *Bilingualism and Special Education: Issues in Assessment and Pedagogy*. San Diego CA: College Hill Press

Daniels, H., Visser, J., Cole, T. and de Reybekill, N. (1999) *Emotional and Behavioural Difficulties in Mainstream Schools*. Research report RR90, London: DfEE

Davies, J. and Brember, I. (1999) 'Reading and mathematics attainments and self-esteem in years 2 and 6: an eight-year cross-sectional study', *Educational Studies*, 25, 145–57.

Dehn, M. (2008) *Working Memory in Academic Learning*, New Jersey: Wiley

Department for Children, Schools and Family (DCSF) (2008) *Handbook for Leading Teachers for Gifted and Talented Education*, Oxfordshire: Nuffield Press

—— (2009) *Statistical First Release: Children Looked After in England*, SFR 25/2009, available online at: http://www.dcsf.gov.uk/rsgateway/DB/SFR/ (retrieved 20 May 2010)

—— *Every Child Matters* (2010) Glossary Term, Children with Additional Needs, available online at: http://www.dcsf.gov.uk/everychildmatters/_glossary/?i_ID=41 (retrieved 15 June 2010)

Department for Education and Employment (DfEE) (2001) *Promoting Children's Mental Health with Early Years and School Settings*, Nottingham: DfEE Publications

Department for Education and Science (1981) *The Education Act*, London: HMSO

Department for Education and Skills (DfES) (2001) *Special Educational Needs: Code of Practice*, Nottingham: DfES Publications

—— (2003) *Raising Standards and Tackling Workload: A National Agreement*, London: DfES Publications

—— (2004) *Every Child Matters: Change for Children*, Nottingham: DfES Publications, available online at: http://education.gov.uk/publications/standard/publication-Detail/Page1/DFES-0012-2006 (retrieved 20 January 2011)

—— (2006) *School Workforce in England (including pupil: teacher ratios and pupil: adult ratios)* (revised), SFR 37/2006, London: DfES Publications

Detweiler, R. E., Hicks, A. P. and Hicks, M. R. (1995) 'The multi-modal diagnosis and treatment of Attention Deficit Hyperactivity Disorder', *Therapeutic Care and Education*, 4 (2), 4–9

Dewey, J. (1933) *How We Think*, Boston MA: DC Heath

Dornyei, Z. (2001) *Teaching and Researching Motivation*, London: Pearson Education Ltd

Dunn, R. and Dunn, K. (1993a) *Teaching Elementary Students through their Individual Learning Styles: Practical Approaches for Grades 3–6*, Boston: Allyn and Bacon

—— (1993b) *Teaching Secondary Students through their Individual Learning Styles: Practical Approaches for Grades 7–12*, Boston, MA: Allyn and Bacon

Dutton, G. (1997) 'Visual problems in children with brain damage', in Shaw, P. (ed.) *Approaches to Working with Children with Multiple Disabilities and a Visual Impairment*, London: on behalf of Vital by RNIB

Dutton, K. (1989) *Writing under Examination Conditions*, Glasgow: Scottish Education Department Regional Psychological Service

Dweck, C. S. (2000) *Self-Theories: Their Role in Motivation, Personality and Development*, Hove: Psychology Press

—— (2008) 'Brainology: transforming students' motivation to learn', *Independent School*, 67 (2), 110–19

—— (2008) *Mindset: The New Psychology of Success*, New York: Ballantine Books

Eastaway, R. and Askew, M. (2010) *Maths for Mums and Dads*, London: Square Peg

Emerson and Hatton (2007) *The Mental Health of Children and Adolescents with Learning Disabilities in Britain*, Lancaster: Lancaster University

Ennis, R. H. (1987) 'A taxonomy of critical thinking dispositions and abilities', in Baron, J. and Sternberg, R. (eds) *Teaching for Thinking*, New York: Freeman

Fox, C. L. and Boulton, M. J. (2006) 'Longitudinal associations between social skills problems and different types of peer victimization', *Violence and Victims*, 21, 387–404

Frey, K. S. and Ruble, D. N. (1985) 'What children say when the teacher is not around: conflicting goals in social comparison and performance assessment in the classroom', *Journal of Personality and Social Psychology*, 48, 550–62

Frith, U. (1985) 'Beneath the surface of developmental dyslexia', in Patterson, K. E., Coltheart, M. and Marshall, J. (eds) *Surface Dyslexia*, London: LEA

Fuchs, D., Fuchs, L. S., Compton, D., Bouton, B., Caffrey, E. and Hill, L. (2007) 'Dynamic assessment as responsiveness to intervention', *Teaching Exceptional Children*, May/June 2007, 58–63

Furman, W., Rahe, D. F. and Hartup, W. W. (1979) 'Rehabilitation of socially withdrawn pre-school children through mixed-age and same-age socialization', *Child Development*, 50, 915–22

Gathercole, S. E. and Alloway, T. P. (2008) *Working Memory and Learning: A Practical Guide for Teachers*, London: Sage

Gibbs, G. (1988) *Learning by Doing: A Guide to Teaching and Learning Methods*, Birmingham: SCED

Goleman, D. (1996) *Emotional Intelligence*, London: Bloomsbury

Good, T. L. and Brophy, J. (1987) *Looking in Classrooms*, 4th edn, New York: Harper & Row

Gosline, A. (2008) 'When kids go bad', *New Scientist*, 12 April 2008, 38–41

Gray, C. (1994) *The Social Story Book*, Arlington VA: Future Horizons

Hall, D. (1995) *Assessing the Needs of Bilingual Pupils: Living in Two Languages*, London: David Fulton

Hall, J. (2005) 'Neuroscience and education', *Topic* 34, November 2005, 67–73

Hallam, S. (2009) 'An evaluation of the Social and Emotional Aspects of Learning (SEAL) programme: promoting positive behaviour, effective learning and well-being in primary school children', *Oxford Review of Education*, 35 (3), 313–30

Hardwick, J. (1996) 'Irregular little beasties', *Special Children, June–July*, 7–10, Birmingham: Questions Publishing.

Harris, J. R. (1997) *The Nurture Assumption*, London: Bloomsbury

Harris, K., Friedlander, B. D., Saddler, B., Remedios, F. and Graham, S. (2005) 'Self-monitoring of attention versus self-monitoring of academic performance', *The Journal of Special Education*, 39 (3), 145–56

Harter, S. (1982) 'The perceived competence scale for children', *Child Development*, 53, 87–97

Hartup, W. (1994) 'Having friends, making friends and keeping friends: relationships as educational contexts', *Emergency Librarian*, January/February 94, 21 (3), 30–32

Hayes, N. (1984) *A First Course in Psychology*, Walton on Thames: Nelson

Haywood, C. H. (2004) 'Thinking in, around and about the curriculum: the role of cognitive education', *International Journal of Disability, Development and Education*, 51 (3), 231–52

Hewett, D. (ed.) (2000) *Challenging Behaviour: Principles and Practices*, London: David Fulton

Hoffman, M. L. (1982) 'Development of prosocial motivation: empathy and guilt', in Eisenberg, N. (ed.) *The Development of Prosocial Behaviour*, New York: Academic Press

Howlin, P., Baron-Cohen, S. and Hadwin, J. (1999) *Teaching Children with Autism to Mind-Read: A Practical Guide*, Chichester: Wiley

Institute for the Future of the Mind (2007), 'Well-being in the classroom', APPG seminar 23 October 2007

Jones, V. and Jones, L. (1995) *Comprehensive Classroom Management*, 4th edn, Boston: Allyn and Bacon

Kagan, S. (1988) *Cooperative Learning: Resources for Teachers*, Riverside CA: University of California Press

Kohn, A. (2000) *Punished by Rewards: The Trouble with Gold Stars, Incentive Plans, A's, Praise and Other Bribes*, Boston: Houghton Mifflin

Koshy, V., Ernest, P. and Casey, R. (2000) *Mathematics for Primary Teachers*, London: Routledge

Kwa, L. (1994) 'Adolescent females' perceptions of competence: what is defined as healthy and achieving', in Gallivan, J., Crozier, S. D. and Lalande, V. M. (eds) *Women, Girls, and Achievement*, North York, Ontario: Captus University Publications

Lawrence, D. (1996) *Enhancing Self-Esteem in the Classroom*, London: Paul Chapman

Leadbetter, J., Morris, S., Timmins, P., Knight, G. and Traxson, D. (1999) *Applying Psychology in the Classroom*, London: David Fulton

Long, M. (2000) *The Psychology of Education*, London: RoutledgeFalmer

Lyon, G. R., Shaywitz, S. E. and Shaywitz, B. A. (2003) 'Defining dyslexia, comorbidity, teachers' knowledge of language and reading', *Annals of Dyslexia*, 53, 1–14

Mannarino, A. P. (1980) 'The development of children's friendships', in Foot, H. C., Chapman, A. J. and Smith, J. R. (eds) *Friendship and Social Relations in Children*, Chichester: Wiley

Masten, A. (2001) 'Ordinary magic: resilience processes in development', *American Psychologist*, 56, 227–38

Matthews, D. and Folsom, C. (2009) 'Making connections: cognition, emotion and a shifting paradigm', in Balchin, T., Hymer, B. and Matthews, D. J. (2009) (eds) *The Routledge International Companion to Gifted Education*, New York: Routledge

Matthews, D. and Foster, J. (2005) *Being Smart about Gifted Children: A Guidebook for Parents and Educators*, Scottsdale, AZ: Great Potential Press

McLinden, M. and Hendrickson, H. (1998) 'Using tactile symbols: a review of current issues', *Approaches to Working with Children with Multiple Disabilities and a Visual Impairment*, London: on behalf of Vital by RNIB

Mead, G. H. (1934) *Mind, Self and Society*, Chicago: University of Chicago Press

Meadows, N. and Melloy, K. J. (1996) 'Behaviour management as a curriculum for students with emotional and behaviour disorders', *Preventing School Failure*, Spring 1996, 40 (3), 124–31

Mellou, E. (1996) 'Can creativity be nurtured in young children?', *Early Child Development and Care*, 119, 119–30

Mesibov, G. B and Howley, M. (2003) *Accessing the Curriculum for Pupils with Autistic Spectrum Disorders: Using the TEACCH Programme to Help Inclusion*, London: David Fulton

Miller, P. H. (1990) 'The development of strategies of selective attention', in Bjorklund, D. F. (ed.) *Children's Strategies: Contemporary Views of Cognitive Development*, Hillsdale NJ: Erlbaum

Moffatt, E. (2001) 'Writing social stories to improve students' social understanding', *GAP*, 2 (1), 12–14

Moon, J. A. (1999) *Reflection in Learning and Professional Development*, London: Kogan Page

Morgan, A. (2007) 'Experiences of a gifted and talented enrichment cluster for pupils aged five to seven', *British Journal of Special Education*, 34 (3), 144–50

Morris, E. (2002) *Excellence Across Sectors*, DfEE Circular 413/98

National Deaf Children's Society (NDCS) (2001) *Understanding Deafness*, London: NDCS Publications

National Oracy Project (1990) *Teaching, Talking and Learning in Key Stage One*, York: National Curriculum Council

Nelson-Jones, R. (1993) *Practical Counselling and Helping Skills*, 3rd edn, London: Cassell

O'Connor, R. D. (1972) 'Relative efficacy of modelling, shaping and the combined procedures for modification of social withdrawal', *Journal of Abnormal Psychology*, 79, 327–34

Ockelford, A. (1998) 'Making sense of the world', in Shaw, P (ed.) *Approaches to Working with Children with Multiple Disabilities and a Visual Impairment*, London: on behalf of Vital by RNIB

Oden, S. and Asher, S. R. (1977) 'Coaching children in social skills for friendship making', *Child Development*, 48, 495–506

Office for Standards in Education (Ofsted) (2005a), 'The annual report of Her Majesty's Chief Inspector of Schools 2003/2004', London: Ofsted

—— (2005b) 'Healthy minds, promoting emotional health and well-being in schools', Reference number HMI 2457, London: Ofsted

—— (2006) 'Improving behaviour: lessons learned from HMI monitoring of secondary schools where behaviour had been judged unsatisfactory', London: Ofsted

Ornstein, P. A., Naus, M. J. and Liberty, C. (1975) 'Rehearsal and organizational processes in children's memory', *Child Development*, 46, 818–30

Parker, J. G. and Asher, S. R. (1987) 'Peer relations and later personal adjustment: are low-accepted children at risk?' *Psychological Bulletin*, 102, 357–89

Pascal, L. (2002) *The Dyslexic in the Classroom*, Special Needs, London: Publishers' Association

Pickard, J. (1999) 'Sense and sensitivity', *People Management*, 28 October 1999, 48–56

Riley, J. (1999) *Teaching Reading at Key Stage 1 and Before*, Cheltenham: Stanley Thornes

Ripley, K., Daines, B. and Barrett, J. (1997) *Dyspraxia: A Guide for Teachers and Parents*, London: David Fulton

Robertson, J. S. (2000) 'Is attribution training a worthwhile classroom intervention for K-12 students with learning difficulties?', *Educational Psychology Review*, 12 (1), 111–34

Robinson, F. P. (1970) *Effective Study*, 4th edn, New York: Harper & Row

Rose, C. (1987) *Accelerated Learning*, Aylesbury: Accelerated Learning Systems

Rosenthal, R. and Jacobson, L. (1966) 'Teachers' expectancies: determinants of pupils' IQ gains', *Psychological Reports*, 19, 115–18

Rowe, C. (1999) 'Do social stories benefit children with autism in mainstream primary school?' *British Journal of Special Education*, 26 (1), 12–14

Rubin, K.H. and Coplan, R. (1992). 'Peer relationships in childhood', in M. Bornstein and M. Lamb (eds) *Developmental Psychology: An advanced textbook*, 3rd edn, Hillsdale NJ: Erlbaum.

Sadker, M. and Sadker, D. (1994) *Failing at Fairness: How America's Schools Cheat Girls*, New York: Scribner

Schachter, F. F. and Strage, A. A. (1982) 'Adults' talk and children's language development', in Moore, S. G. and Cooper, C. R. (eds) *The Young Child: Reviews of Research*, vol. III, Washington DC: National Association for the Education of Young Children

Schoenfeld, N. A., Rutherford Jr, R. B., Gable, R. A. and Rock, M. L. (2008) 'ENGAGE: a blueprint for incorporating social skills training into daily academic instruction', *Preventing School Failure*, 52 (3), 17–27

Selman, R. L. and Jaquette, D. (1977) 'Stability and oscillation in interpersonal awareness: a clinical-developmental analysis', in Keasey, C. B. (ed.) *The Nebraska Symposium on Motivation*, XXV, Lincoln NE: University of Nebraska Press

Sharp, C. (2004) 'Developing young children's creativity: what can we learn from research?', *Topic*, Autumn 2004, Issue 32, 5–12

Shenk, D. (2010a) *Does the Gifted Label get in the Way of Developing Real Potential?*, available online at: http://learning.blogs.nytimes.com/2010/03/12/teacher-q-does-the-gifted-label-get-in-the-way-of-developing-real-potential/ (retrieved: 24 June 2010)

—— (2010b) *The Genius in All of Us: Why Everything You've Been Told About Genetics, Talent and IQ is wrong*, New York: Doubleday

Shevin, M. and Klein, N. K. (1984) 'The importance of choice-making skills for students with severe disabilities', *The Association for Persons with Severe Handicaps*, 9 (3), 159–66

Sigelman, C. K. and Shaffer, D. R. (1991) *Life-Span Human Development*, Monterey CA: Brooks Cole

Smith, C. (2001) 'Using social stories with children with autistic spectrum disorders: an evaluation', *Good Autism Practice*, 2 (1), 16–25

Smith, P. K., Cowie, H. and Blades, M. (1998) *Understanding Children's Development*, 3rd edn, Oxford: Blackwell

Snow, C. E. (1977) 'The development of conversation between mothers and babies', *Journal of Child Language*, 4, 1–22

Snow, C. E. and Ferguson, C. A. (eds) (1977) *Talking to Children*, Cambridge: Cambridge University Press

Special Children (2000a) 'Dyspraxia – at a glance', *Special Children*, 129, May, 22

—— (2000b) 'ADHD – at a glance', *Special Children*, 130, June–July, 36

—— (2000c) 'Dyslexia – at a glance', *Special Children*, 132, October, 28

—— (2001a) 'Down's syndrome – at a glance', *Special Children*, 134, January, 33

—— (2001b) 'Autistic spectrum disorder – at a glance', *Special Children*, 136, March, 37

Starr, J. (2008) *The Coaching Manual*, London: Pearson

Stipek, D. J. (1988) *Motivation to Learn: From Theory to Practice*, New Jersey: Prentice Hall

The Poverty Site (2009) *Looked After Children*, available online at: http://www.poverty.org.uk/29/index.shtml (retrieved 22 June 2010)

Thomson, M. (1990) *Developmental Dyslexia*, 3rd edn, London: Whurr

Tuckman, B. and Jensen, N. (1977) 'Stages of small group development revisited', *Group and Organizational Studies*, 2, 419–27

Watson, C. (1995) 'Helping families from other cultures decide on how to talk to their child with language delay', *Wig Wag*, Winter, 1995

Wentzel, K. R., Barry, C. M. and Caldwell, K. A. (2004) 'Friendships in middle school: influences on motivation and school adjustment', *Journal of Educational Psychology*, 96, 195–203

Wolin, S., (2004) 'Presenting a resiliency paradigm for teachers', in Waxman, H. Padron, Y. and Gray, J. (eds) *Educational Resiliency: Student, Teacher and School Perspectives*, 189–204, Greenwich CT: Information Age

World Health Organization (WHO) (2007) *International Statistical Classification of Diseases and Related Health Problems, 10th Revision Version for 2007*, Geneva: WHO

Wragg, E. C. and Brown, G. (1993) *Explaining in the Primary School*, London: Routledge

Index

Taylor & Francis

eBooks

FOR LIBRARIES

ORDER YOUR
FREE 30 DAY
INSTITUTIONAL
TRIAL TODAY!

Over 22,000 eBook titles in the Humanities,
Social Sciences, STM and Law from some of the
world's leading imprints.

Choose from a range of subject packages or create your own!

Benefits for
you

▶ Free MARC records
▶ COUNTER-compliant usage statistics
▶ Flexible purchase and pricing options

Benefits
for your
user

▶ Off-site, anytime access via Athens or referring URL
▶ Print or copy pages or chapters
▶ Full content search
▶ Bookmark, highlight and annotate text
▶ Access to thousands of pages of quality research
  at the click of a button

For more information, pricing enquiries or to order
a free trial, contact your local online sales team.

UK and Rest of World: **online.sales@tandf.co.uk**
US, Canada and Latin America:
e-reference@taylorandfrancis.com

www.ebooksubscriptions.com

 Taylor & Francis **eBooks**
Taylor & Francis Group

ALPSP Award for
BEST eBOOK
PUBLISHER
2009 Finalist

A flexible and dynamic resource for teaching, learning and research.